CIRCLES®

A Culturally Appropriate Preschool Curriculum for American Indian Children

CIRCLES A Culturally Appropriate Preschool Curriculum for American Indian Children
Book 1: The Core Curriculum Approach –
© 2017 National Center for Families Learning. All rights reserved. Printed in the United States of America. Cover photo credit: Blackwater Community School FACE Program, Preschool Classroom. No part of this book may be used or reproduced in any manner whatsoever without written permission except in the case of brief quotations embodied in critical articles and reviews. For information address National Center for Families Learning, 325 West Main Street, Suite 300, Louisville, KY 40202.

familieslearning.org

First Edition

ISBN - 978-0-9987116-3-8

CIRCLES®

A Culturally Appropriate Preschool Curriculum for American Indian Children

Book 1: **The Core Curriculum Approach**

This curriculum and its supporting materials were a collaborative effort. Content development and editorial services were provided by the following NCFL staff:

Principal writer

    Kim Jacobs

Content contributors and internal review

    Marilyn Box
    Margo Waddell
    Cathy Miller
    Jessica Dilworth
    Cotillion Sneddy

Editor

    Gail Price

Subject matter expertise, materials review, content writing, and support were provided by:

    Education Staff at the National Center for Families Learning

Content feedback on materials provided by preschool teachers and co-teachers in the following Bureau of Indian Education schools:

    Baca/Dlo'ay azhi Community School
    Blackwater Community School
    Enemy Swim Day School
    Fond du Lac Ojibwe School
    John F. Kennedy School
    Lac Courte Oreilles Ojibwe School
    Little Singer Community School
    Oneida Nation Community School
    Salt River Elementary School
    St. Francis Indian Schools
    To'Hajiillee Community School

Sharon Darling is the President and Founder of the National Center for Families Learning

© 2017 National Center for Families Learning

CONTENTS

CIRCLES® A Culturally Appropriate Preschool Curriculum for American Indian Children i

Components of an effective curriculum iii

Overview 1

Chapter 1 Focus on Child Development and Best Practice 7

Chapter 2 The CIRCLES® Frameworks 15

Chapter 3 Culture and Learning Styles 25
    Checklist for a Family and Culture Rich Preschool Environment 36

Chapter 4 The Teaching Strategies 37

Chapter 5 The Classroom Environment 43
    Building Community 44
    The Room Arrangement 52
    Choosing Materials 57
    CIRCLES® Classroom Environment Checklist 66

Chapter 6 The Morning Routine 69
    The CIRCLES® Morning Routine 72
    Segments of the Daily Routine 73
    Arrival and Departure 73
    Circle Time Small Group Time 76
    Wonder–Work–Share 85
    Parent and Child Together (PACT) Time 94
    Daily Routine Checklist 101

Chapter 7 Planning for Children 103
    Assessment to Instruction 103
    Observation 108
    Lesson Planning in Circles 111
    CIRCLES® Early Childhood Learning Domains 114
    CIRCLES® Learning Domain Checklist 132
    CIRCLES® Daily/Weekly Lesson Plan 141
    CIRCLES® Daily/Weekly At-a-Glance 143
    CIRCLES® Daily/Weekly (Sample/Detailed) 144

Chapter 8 CIRCLES® Curriculum Application 157

CIRCLES® Curriculum Application Sequence At-a-Glance 159

CIRCLES® Curriculum Application Sequence Implementation Guidance 164

References 188

The National Center for Families Learning

Literacy is at the root of a person's ability to succeed, and the family is at the heart.

Since 1989, the National Center for Families Learning (NCFL) has helped more than one million families make educational and economic progress by pioneering—and continuously improving—family literacy and family learning programs.

Our emphasis is on family literacy for a simple reason—study after study shows that family, home, and community are the true drivers of a child's education. The family literacy approach harnesses the strength of parent-child bonds to help those who are most at risk of failing economically, emotionally, and socially. We build success by strengthening their confidence, increasing their ability, and broadening their outlook. The results have an impact on a personal level as well as a national one.

NCFL views education as a family affair. We see every parent as an asset; every family as a resource. By working together, we help families create their own learning networks. Whether it is obtaining a high school credential, reading on grade level, or pursuing higher education, the results pave the way for economic self-sufficiency and propel families toward achieving their dreams, and our country toward collective success. Since 1991, more than 2 million families in more than 100 communities across the country have been impacted by programs developed by NCFL—our team has pioneered the concept of families learning and serving together to raise literacy levels and improve communities.

Vision and Mission

The National Center for Families Learning exists to eradicate poverty through educational solutions. With educators and literacy advocates, NCFL provides resources that empower and raise families to achieve their potential.

Who We Serve

NCFL's tools and services can benefit all families. Our primary focus is to empower parents and children living in poverty and struggling with low literacy and language skills to improve their lives and become strong contributors to society.

What We Do

NCFL advances literacy and education by developing, implementing, and documenting innovative and promising two-generation practices, networks, and learning tools.

Our Partners

We lead and work with learners, administrators, teachers, librarians, policymakers, philanthropists, and advocates.

Our Expertise:

- Literacy content areas, spanning early childhood to adult learning, with particular emphasis on reading and lifelong learning
- Program design and execution, with particular emphasis on innovative two-generation approaches to literacy and learning
- Learning communities and digital learning for students, families and educators
- Leadership, advocacy, and professional services

Visit our website at familieslearning.org

CIRCLES® A CULTURALLY APPROPRIATE PRESCHOOL CURRICULUM FOR AMERICAN INDIAN CHILDREN

The foundational aspects of the CIRCLES® Curriculum are grounded in evidence-based practices and principles, with a strong focus on Native culture and language preservation, and early childhood best practice. Learning styles vary from child to child. Research provides us with evidence of learning styles and strategies that best support American Indian children's learning, growth, and development. Within the CIRCLES approach, teachers are encouraged to use a variety of teaching strategies to support various approaches to learning, with attention to child observation and assessment that informs and guides instructional practices. Twenty-seven years of working with American Indian preschool children and families have contributed to and shaped this unique curriculum approach created by the National Center for Families Learning (NCFL).

The following approaches to learning form the **CIRCLES® Teaching Strategy:**

- *A global or holistic style*—for the organization of information
- *A visual style*—for mentally representing information
- *A reflective style*—for processing information, and
- *A collaborative approach*—for completing tasks (Hilberg & Tharp, 2002).

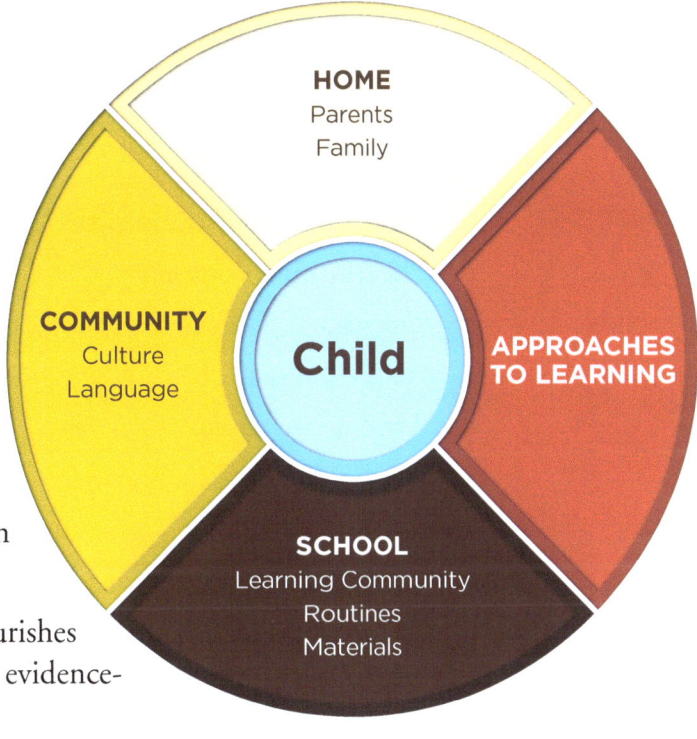

The CIRCLES Curriculum approach is based on these foundational principles:

- A balanced approach to preschool that nourishes children's wonder and creativity within an evidence- and standards-based curriculum
- Culturally responsive instruction that addresses the prominent learning styles of American Indian children
- A strong focus on family engagement that impacts academic achievement
- Evidence-based language and literacy practices that support both the child's Native language and skill development in English.

For more information about the **CIRCLES Curriculum, CIRCLES Professional Development**, or to bring the CIRCLES Curriculum to your American Indian early childhood/preschool program, please contact Kim Jacobs, National Center for Families Learning, or by email at kjacobs@familieslearning.org.

Hilberg. R. S. & Tharp. R. G. (2002). *Theoretical perspectives, research findings, and classroom implications of the learning styles of American Indian and Alaska Native students.* (ERIC Document Reproduction Services No. ED 468000)

CIRCLES® Curriculum Materials Include:

Book 1: **CIRCLES® The Core Curriculum Approach**

Book 2: **CIRCLES® Language & Literacy Development in Preschool**

Book 3: **CIRCLES® Family Engagement in Preschool**

Content Included in the Curriculum Materials:

- Three Curriculum Frameworks
    - Program Framework
    - Teaching Framework
    - Learning Framework
- Seven Curriculum Elements
    - Culture & Learning Styles
    - The Teaching Strategy
    - The Classroom Environment
    - The Morning Routine
    - Language & Literacy Development
    - Family Engagement
    - Planning for Children
- Curriculum Application Guidance
    - Evidence-based strategies
    - Sample lesson plans
    - Easy to understand Learning Domains for three- to five-year old children
    - Teacher self-assessment checklists
    - Preschool developmental checklists
    - Quarterly implementation guidance
    - Family engagement strategies

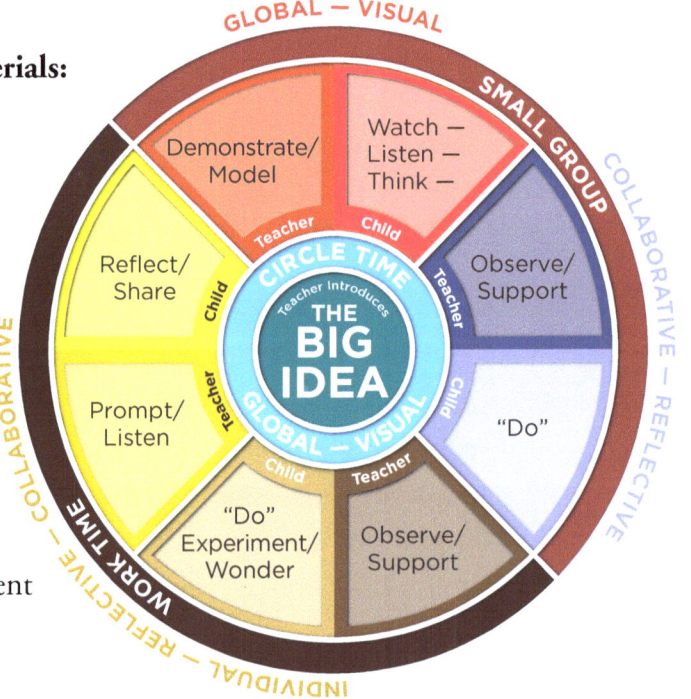

Professional Development:

- Designed to fit the needs of your program
- Includes:
    - Written curriculum materials
    - On-site Professional Development
    - Online Professional Development & Support
    - Technical Assistance & Coaching
    - Family Event Support

COMPONENTS OF AN EFFECTIVE CURRICULUM

Components of an Effective Curriculum*	CIRCLES® Curriculum Elements and Evidence
Curriculum Essentials	***The CIRCLES Program Framework lays the foundational groundwork*** for teaching and learning in preschool. It addresses how the *child learns and is taught* within his or her own *home, school,* and *community*. The CIRCLES curriculum approach is the result of over 27 years of evidence working with American Indian children and families, and includes these four essentials: • ***A balanced approach*** to preschool that nourishes children's wonder and creativity within an evidence- and standards-based curriculum • ***Culturally responsive instruction*** that addresses the prominent learning styles of American Indian children • A strong focus on ***family engagement*** that impacts academic achievement • ***Evidence-based language and literacy practices*** that support both the child's Native language and skill development in English. [See CIRCLES Curriculum Frameworks]
Curriculum is grounded in child development principles and best practice	***The CIRCLES Curriculum Elements are those essential and intentional focuses of learning*** that happen every day in the classroom. The elements are made up of evidence-based strategies and early childhood best practice. Each individual element can stand on its own—but when all seven are combined collectively within a program, the results are powerful. Together, these seven elements are the core of the CIRCLES Curriculum. The seven Curriculum Elements include: 1. Culture & Learning Styles 2. The Teaching Strategy 3. The Classroom Environment 4. The Morning Routine 5. Language & Literacy Skill Development 6. Family Engagement 7. Planning for Children ***CIRCLES is grounded in foundational early childhood best practice:*** • *Teach all children, regardless of their abilities or approaches to learning* • *Young children learn best through play* • *Adults—parents and teachers—maintain realistic expectations for children* • *Children learn best through active learning* • *Provide consistency in routines and habits* • *Create a supportive learning community* • *Maintain a clean and safe learning environment* • *Create a warm and welcome environment for families.* "While no single curriculum or pedagogical approach can be identified as best, children who attend well-planned, high-quality early childhood programs in which curriculum aims are specified and integrated across domains, tend to learn more and are better prepared…" (Bowman, Donovan and Burns, 2001, p. 7-8). [See CIRCLES Introduction, Curriculum Elements]

Continued on next page

Components Of An Effective Curriculum

Curriculum is research-based and shows effects of child outcomes	*The CIRCLES Curriculum approach is based on 27 years of practice* working in early childhood education in American Indian preschools in the Family and Child Education (FACE) program, and the evaluation reports of those program years; the current evidence supporting how preschool children best learn to read and be ready for kindergarten entry; research-based strategies that support parent engagement and academic achievement; and a wide review of the literature/evidence that supports American Indian children's learning styles. *[See CIRCLES Introduction, Culture & Learning Styles, References]* • Preschool children's expressive vocabulary and oral language scores significantly and meaningfully increased to the 55th national percentile within one year, 2 standard scores above the national average (Research & Training Associates**, 2015). • Preschool children with an IEP are half as likely to require special education services at kindergarten entry (RTA, 2010). Preschoolers made meaningful progress in closing the gap and reaching the national average (RTA, 2015). • Children scored significantly higher on kindergarten reading and math assessments than did children who did not participate in the curriculum approach (RTA, 2015). • Preschool children demonstrate significant improvement in ratings on every learning domain for 3- and 4-year-old children (RTA, 2015).
Curriculum represents depth of each learning domain with specific learning goals and objectives	*The CIRCLES Teaching Framework represents specific Approaches to Learning plus seven Early Childhood Learning Domains* aligned with common philosophies of Native culture. Those domains of learning are: • Language and Literacy • Math • Science • Social Studies • Social-Emotional Development • Physical Development • Creative Arts *[See CIRCLES Early Childhood Learning Domains, 3-5 Years]*
Curriculum has well-designed lesson plans and learning activities.	*The CIRCLES Daily Lesson Plan is designed to facilitate intentional teaching using active and engaged learning strategies, balancing both child-led and teacher directed experiences.* On a weekly basis, the preschool teacher and co-teacher meet to plan the next week's lessons. Teachers review the current week, discuss what went well and what adjustments need to be made. Observations of student performance, recorded anecdotal notes, and collected work samples drive the planning discussion. From this observation and assessment data, teachers choose goals/objectives from the CIRCLES Learning Domains (or state/federal standards) and create their lesson plans using the CIRCLES Daily Lesson Plan. Sample Lesson Plans are provided for teachers. *[See Curriculum Elements: Planning for Children]*

Continued on next page

Components Of An Effective Curriculum

Curriculum supports language and literacy development and kindergarten readiness	*High-quality preschool learning environments are respectful and supportive of children's Native culture and language* and will simultaneously increase English language skills. The National Early Literacy Panel (NELP), a group of researchers charged with the task of determining the best predictors for preschool children's success in learning how to read, reviewed hundreds of evidence-based research studies to share the important concepts for teachers to incorporate into their teaching. NCFL worked directly with the NELP and created a practitioner guide to the NELP findings, titled *What Works: An Introductory Teacher Guide for Early Language and Emergent Literacy Instruction*. This guide, included in the CIRCLES Curriculum, provides the basis for language and literacy instruction. In CIRCLES, we focus on the four predictor skills identified by the NELP: - *Oral language development* - *Phonological Awareness* - *Alphabet Knowledge/Print Concepts* - *Writing.* *The CIRCLES Curriculum has a strong focus on reading and parent support of children's reading development.* Parents are taught the same strategies as teachers so both can support children's reading and oral language development. On average, student vocabulary, language and comprehension scores increased from the 7th percentile to the 45th percentile in 2005; from the 23rd to the 45th percentile in 2010; and increased from the 37th to the 61st percentile in 2015, above the national average and showing consistent gains (RTA, 2005, 2010, 2015). *[See Curriculum Element: Language & Literacy Development]*
Curriculum supports responsive teaching	*The CIRCLES Curriculum is designed to provide a balance of child-focused and teacher-directed experiences*, using a variety of teaching strategies to support children's learning per individual learning styles, approaches to learning, needs and interests, and academic goals. Parents influence and input is valued and included in instructional planning. There are times built into the daily routine for children's individual, small group, and large group play and work, with adult supportive, responsive strategies recommended for best practice. *[See Curriculum Elements, Daily Routine, Environment, Planning for Children]*

Continued on next page

Components Of An Effective Curriculum

Curriculum supports individualized instruction	***The CIRCLES approach has a large focus on early intervention,*** utilizing an ongoing screening and referral process. In FACE, the percentage of children who received screening services increased from less than 40% in 1994 to over 93% in 2015. Early detection and intervention is critical in providing special needs services for children for them to be successful by kindergarten entry. Preschool children who participated are half as likely to have an Individualized Education Program (IEP) at school entry, as did children who did not participate (RTA, 2015). Individualized instruction is intentional when planning for children, particularly when planning lesson plans for Small Group Time. The afternoon section of the daily routine is left open for teachers to plan focused instruction based on the needs of the children. *[See Curriculum Elements, Planning for Children]*
Curriculum supports culturally and linguistically responsive education	***Native language and culture is embedded within the CIRCLES curriculum.*** Preschool teachers infuse culture and language into multiple aspects of the children's day. Teachers make connections with the culture and language teachers at their schools, elders in their communities, or integrate on their own. Parents and families provide essential information. Strategies vary from school to school and tribe to tribe to be culturally relevant. The CIRCLES approach strives to fit with the needs of the community, and not vice versa. Learning styles of all children vary and there are patterns of learning styles that often best support American Indian children. Teachers are encouraged to use a variety of learning strategies and observation to inform instructional practices. The prominent learning styles that form the *CIRCLES Teaching Strategy* include: • A global or holistic style—for the organization of information • A visual style—for mentally representing information • A reflective style—for processing information, and • A collaborative approach—for completing tasks (Hilberg & Tharp, 2002). *[See Curriculum Elements – Culture & Learning Styles, The Teaching Strategy]*
Curriculum provides methods of ongoing assessment	***Assessing children's development and learning is essential in the CIRCLES Curriculum.*** Assessing children's abilities, developing appropriate curriculum, and planning for daily instruction are all part of the assessment to instruction process. Assessment is essential to curriculum and provides a basis for planning instruction, communicating with parents, identifying children's needs and goals, and evaluating program impact. The CIRCLES approach recommends an authentic assessment system that includes observation, screening, an oral language test, developmental checklists, and a formal developmental assessment. *[See Curriculum Elements: Planning for Children]*

Continued on next page

Components Of An Effective Curriculum

Curriculum provides professional development opportunities	*NCFL provides standard and customized professional development options for the CIRCLES Curriculum approach to meet the needs of your school or program.* Our research-based professional development options include: • On-site professional development • Online professional development courses • Technical Assistance and Coaching (on-site and distance) NCFL has provided high-quality, research-based professional development to educators for over 28 years.
Curriculum provides family engagement support and materials	*Family engagement is an essential element of the CIRCLES curriculum approach.* Significantly more parents report that they read to their children daily or almost daily as a result of their participation in programs with this approach. Seventy-nine percent of parents report they continue to read to their K-3 children on a daily basis. Family engagement is a direct predictor of expressive language performance at preschool exit and expressive language is the largest direct predictor of kindergarten entry performance (RTA, 2015). Seventy-six percent of parents report they read to their child on a *daily* or *almost daily* basis. A significantly higher 80% reported doing so at the end of the year (RTA, 2015)

*Components modified from Preschool Curriculum Consumer Report, The National Center of Quality Teaching and Learning, Office of Head Start.

**Research & Training Associates (RTA) is the outside evaluator for the Family and Child Education (FACE) program. RTA has conducted the outside evaluations of the program since 1990 with 26 years of collective data attributed to the success of the program.

OVERVIEW

Since 1990, the National Center for Families Learning has worked with American Indian schools to promote school readiness, adult college and career readiness, and family learning. Utilizing a two-generation approach, NCFL has worked alongside the Bureau of Indian Education (BIE)—the funder for these school programs—to impact teacher quality through professional development, increase children's language and literacy development to better prepare them for kindergarten, and support parents through parent education and adult education services.

The work of NCFL with American Indian children and families has primarily been done through the Family and Child Education (FACE) program. Initiated in 1990 and designed as an integrated model for early childhood and parent involvement for American Indian families, FACE programs have succeeded in addressing achievement gaps for American Indian children by better preparing them for school. The goals of the FACE program are to:

- Support parents/primary caregivers in their role as their child's first and most influential teacher.
- Strengthen family-school-community connections.
- Increase parent participation in their child's learning and expectations for academic achievement.
- Support and celebrate the unique cultural and linguistic diversity of each American Indian community served by the program.
- Promote lifelong learning.

During the 27-year history of FACE, the program has served 44,743 American Indians, including 20,932 adults and 23,811 children (RTA, 2015). Over the course of the program years, adults and children participated in FACE services for an average of two program years. For preschool children, the evaluation data clearly shows areas of growth in identifying children for developmental delays, referring services for children with special needs, reducing the number of IEPs needed at Kindergarten entry, increasing expressive language development and Kindergarten readiness.

You can find out more about the FACE program by visiting the Bureau of Indian Education's or the National Center for Families Learning's websites.

This curriculum—***CIRCLES: A Culturally Appropriate Preschool Curriculum for American Indian Children***—is designed for all American Indian preschoolers and can be adapted to fit any American Indian school and community. It is designed to provide high-quality and developmentally appropriate preschool experiences, grounded in the context of each child's unique culture and native language.

The CIRCLES approach is based on four basic tenets:

- Balanced approach to preschool that nourishes children's wonder and creativity, yet addresses standards and data-driven instructional practices
- Culturally responsive teaching strategies that support varied learning styles
- Strong and intentional family engagement component
- Strong focus on language and literacy development in the home language and in English to support kindergarten readiness.

Lessons learned and knowledge gained from years of working with American Indian preschool children and their families have contributed to the development of this preschool curriculum. The foundational aspects of the curriculum are grounded in evidence-based principles (American Indian learning styles and culture, parent engagement, and language and literacy development), and are inclusive of early childhood best practices.

Our goal is to inform teachers who work with American Indian preschool children of the best practices that meet the needs of all children in the classroom—and provide appropriate curriculum guidance to design early childhood environments, daily routines, and lesson planning, that are culturally relevant and sensitive to American Indian learning styles.

The end result is to successfully prepare American Indian children for school, while preserving their Native language and cultural traditions.

The CIRCLES Curriculum Approach – An evidence-based FAQ

The FACE program is evaluated annually by an outside evaluator that provides an annual report to the Bureau of Indian Education. The responses to the questions that follow represent information collected from these evaluation reports. You can find out more about these evaluation reports by visiting face.familieslearning.org

1. **What is the evidence that the CIRCLES curriculum approach prepares three- and four-year-old children for kindergarten?**

    The evidence exists in several areas—children's English language and vocabulary development, support for children with special needs, and overall school readiness.

Findings from two Impact Studies (RTA 2004, 2008) indicate that the program improves children's school readiness through its direct, significant, and meaningful impacts on preschool attendance, the number of books and literacy resources in the home, and increased home literacy activity.

Children enter the FACE preschool program scoring far below the national average in expressive language development. They also enter below the national percentile rank. FACE preschool children with special needs score significantly below the national average at school entry (pre-test). At post-test, they score near the national average, thereby diminishing the need for costly, long-term special education.

More specifically, FACE children who experience this curriculum approach enter at the 30th national percentile rank. After attending a full year of preschool, they score at the 55th national percentile—which renders them on a level playing field with children nationally.

An additional year of preschool increases the percentage of children who attend with high frequency and score at or above the national average—from 36% to 50% of preschoolers.

2. **Would the CIRCLES curriculum approach be appropriate for widespread adoption in more tribal communities?**

   The CIRCLES curriculum approach is inclusive of families and culture. CIRCLES provides a developmentally and culturally responsive curriculum model that can be adapted to fit any American Indian preschool program. The curriculum has a proven track record with preschool children who reside in rural, urban, high poverty, and high needs areas to better prepare them for successful kindergarten entry.

   The CIRCLES preschool curriculum is the result of over 27 years of lessons learned working with American Indian and high-needs children/families and specifically includes:

   - A family engagement approach to preschool education that focuses on the child and the family. This is a developmentally appropriate and balanced approach to school readiness that nourishes children's wonder and creativity within the context of an evidence- and standards-based curriculum.
   - A culturally relevant approach to the preservation of Native language and culture, infused within the curriculum.
   - A strong and intentional focus on preschool children's English language and literacy development and outcomes, embedded within the evidence-based curriculum.
   - A strong and intentional focus on parent/family engagement that supports children's learning and academic achievement.

   Native language and culture is embedded within the CIRCLES curriculum. Preschool teachers infuse culture and language into as many aspects of the day as possible. Teachers make connections with the culture and language teachers at their schools, elders in their communities, or integrate on their own. Strategies vary from school to school and tribe to tribe to be culturally relevant.

3. **Does the CIRCLES curriculum approach increase vocabulary of dual language learners?**

   The CIRCLES curriculum positively affects the English language development and vocabulary of three- and four-year-old children. CIRCLES uses evidence-based strategies and culturally appropriate learning styles that target all domains of learning, particularly language, speech, and vocabulary development. The use of dialogic reading is one of many strategies that produces results. As measured by the nationally normed Expressive One Word Picture Vocabulary Test, children have made significant gains. In fact, children leave FACE preschool with *significant* and *meaningful* increases in expressive language.

   FACE children enter preschool below the national norm but leave with significant gains, regardless of whether children attend preschool for one semester or the full year.

   These gains also relate to attendance. For each year of preschool attended, children *significant* and *meaningful* increase their expressive language development; however, children with low attendance remain below average. Children with moderate attendance reach the national average, and children with high attendance make significant gains, above the national average in expressive language. A focus on attendance and retention of students is critical to their overall success.

   In short, the higher the children's attendance rates (and thus more exposure to the curriculum), the greater the gains in expressive language.

4. **Is the CIRCLES curriculum approach effective in service to children with special needs?**

   This approach has a large focus on early detection. The percentage of children who have received screening services has increased from less than 40% in 1994 to over 93% in 2015. Early detection and intervention is critical in providing special needs services for children, for them to be successful by kindergarten. In fact, the success of the program is demonstrated by the finding that preschool children who participated are half as likely to have an Individualized Education Program (IEP) at school entry, as did children who did not participate.

   In 2012, 10% of the preschool children enrolled had an IEP. FACE preschool children with IEPs scored significantly below other preschoolers at pre-test (school entry) and scored almost a full standard deviation below the national average (i.e. standard score of 86). At post-test, they scored similarly to their preschoolers with an average post-test score of 98—near the national average, thereby leveling the playing field for children who had been identified early for special needs, again eliminating the need for costly, long-term special education.

5. Is there evidence that parents are more involved in their children's education at home?

Parent reports suggest that FACE participation impacts their home literacy practices.

- Significantly more parents reported that they read to their children daily or almost daily because of their FACE participation.

- Seventy-nine percent of FACE parents reported they also read to their K-3 children daily. This is a considerably higher percentage than parents nationwide report, with only 36% of parents nationally read to their K-3 children this frequently.

- FACE parents significantly increased the frequency that they listen to their children read by year's end. Eighty-nine percent of FACE parents reported listening to their children read daily at the end of FACE participation.

- The frequency that FACE parents tell stories to their children significantly increased during FACE participation. At the end of the year, 77% of parents compared with 70% of parents early in their FACE participation reported that they tell stories to their children daily or almost daily.

Focus on Child Development and Best Practice

Preschool education within a family-focused and culturally responsive learning environment is designed to promote preschool children's learning, growth, and development, as well as to engage parents and support their roles in their children's learning.

It is important for both teachers and parents to know basic child development principles to understand how typical preschool children learn best, and to understand the realistic learning expectations for three- and four-year-old children. Having unrealistic expectations for children's performance, learning, and behavior can often prove detrimental to children, and can make teachers' and parents' jobs more difficult.

Children's physical, cognitive, and social-emotional skills develop in many ways—through active exploration and investigation, personal discovery, rich learning environments, meaningful interactions with peers and adults, and opportunities to develop language skills within meaningful contexts. Partnerships with parents, along with a respect for the culture of the families and cultural inclusion, are not only important, but also necessary. Children grow and develop best in learning environments that not only celebrate, but also embrace the important role of parents, and the essential teachings of their culture.

The domains of children's development—cognitive, physical, and social-emotional—are closely related. Each domain influences and is influenced by the other domains. They are often categorized in the following ways:

Physical development addresses the changes and growth in the physical body, as well as the functioning of body systems. Brain development, physiological development, large and small motor development, and physical health and nutrition are integral to this domain.

> The domains of children's development—cognitive, physical, and social-emotional—are closely related. Each domain influences and is influenced by the other domains.

Cognitive development addresses the developmental range of mental processes and abilities, including brain functioning, perception, attention, memory, academic learning and everyday knowledge, thinking, listening, speaking, problem solving, imagination and creativity.

Social-Emotional development addresses the development of emotional and social abilities focused on interactions with ourselves and others, including self-understanding, emotions, interpersonal skills, friendships and intimate relationships, and moral reasoning and behavior.

"Cognitive, social-emotional mental health, and physical development are complementary, mutually supportive areas of growth, all requiring active attention in the pre-school years. Social skills and physical dexterity influence cognitive development, just as cognition plays a role in children's social understanding and motor competence. All are therefore related to early learning and later academic achievement and are necessary domains of early childhood pedagogy…. While no single curriculum or pedagogical approach can be identified as best, children who attend well-planned, high-quality early childhood programs in which curriculum aims are specified and integrated across domains, tend to learn more and are better prepared to master the complex domains of formal schooling… Children who have a broad base of experiences in domain-specific knowledge move more rapidly in acquiring more complex skills" (Bowman, Donovan and Burns, 2001, p. 7-8).

Children develop according to certain established principles. All children go through developmental stages in the same chronological manner but not necessarily at the same rate. There are ranges in normal development that allow for these differences. Development occurs in a relatively orderly sequence, with later abilities, skills, and knowledge building on those already acquired. Development does follow a well-defined path—from the simple to the complex and from the general to the specific. Physical development proceeds from the head down, and from near to far (head-to-feet and trunk-to-fingers/toes). Cognitive development proceeds along predictable and orderly lines. Although many child development theorists describe the stages of cognitive development in different ways, they agree that development always occurs in sequence, although the timing of the stages may vary.

Understanding where preschool children are in these sequences and stages helps the teacher plan the appropriate learning experiences for individuals and groups of children, and provide them in a developmentally appropriate way.

But just understanding child development is not enough. Teachers must observe and assess children so they can determine their strengths and abilities, their interests and goals, and their areas for growth. As well, teachers should make efforts to know and understand the child's home environment and culture, including the language(s) spoken in the home. Development and learning are influenced by social and cultural contexts. Children develop and learn best in the context of a community where they are safe and valued, their physical needs are met, and they feel psychologically secure.

Who are your preschoolers?

Children ages three-to-five years are rapidly growing little beings who are starting to explore and understand their world in a wider arena. They may change their minds often, but see their own viewpoint very clearly (and express it!). They are literal and thrive upon success.

Preschool children are still learning the social graces and often their actions speak louder than their words. Although preschoolers can be busy and loud in their learning, they like their quiet and alone times too. They trust easily, laugh a lot, and say what they think—sometimes candidly so! They usually don't mind a mess, especially if they are cutting, gluing, and drawing—and often learn through the messes and mistakes they make. Manipulating materials is necessary for them when learning—they need to hold, tear, twist, draw, put together, and take apart.

When teaching young preschoolers, it is important to know that 10 minutes is a very long time. They prefer short, simple and varied activities. Play is their most important avenue for learning.

> **Preschool teachers know and understand the strengths and abilities of the children in their classroom community. Preparing for each individual child, every day, is the first defense in knowing what and how to teach.**

Best Practice

When teaching preschool children, keep in mind the following best practices:
- Teach all children, regardless of their abilities or approaches to learning
- Young children learn best through play
- Adults—parents and teachers—maintain realistic expectations for growing and developing children
- Children learn best through active learning strategies
- Provide consistency in daily routines and habits
- Create a supportive learning community
- Maintain a clean and safe learning environment
- Create a warm, welcoming, and engaging environment for families

Teaching all children

The experiences provided, and the materials used in most preschool classrooms, are designed to meet the needs and abilities of many children. When experiences do not meet the specific needs and interests of a child, they can be adapted or expanded to accommodate that child's individual needs. This includes accommodating for a child's preferred learning styles. Adaptations allow children to use their current skills while promoting the acquisition of new skills. They can make the difference between children merely being present and being actively engaged.

Through ongoing observation and assessment, preschool teachers reflect and plan the best ways to ensure appropriate educational and developmental experiences for all young children—regardless of their unique abilities. Just as each child is different, methods and strategies to work with young children vary.

Realistic expectations

The methods and strategies for preschool children are not the same as teaching elementary students. Preschoolers learn from hands-on, active experiences that allow them to manipulate, use, and explore materials and situations. They learn from social activities, such as in the House and Block Areas of the classroom, as well as from small and large group instruction. Preschool teachers understand the growth and development of children this age and teach according to what they can realistically expect children to do at this stage of their lives. Preschool children do not learn and thrive when sitting at desks, during "drill and skill" sessions, or while doing repetitive and uninteresting worksheets. They learn and thrive when the learning is interesting, hands-on, and active.

Children learn through play, and play is their work.

Learning through play

Children learn through play, and play is their work. Through exploration and playful interactions with peers, preschool children broaden their knowledge and build understanding about the world around them.

Play is also a social activity in which involvement with others varies. Some children simply watch others play (on-looking play), some play by themselves (solitary play), some play side-by-side others (parallel play), and some play with others (associative/cooperative play).

Whatever the involvement with others, when children engage in play they are entering into a magical world of their own making, one in which they conjure up their own ideas and problems, make their own decisions, and plan their own work. During this engagement, children are provided with the prime opportunity to practice new skills in many domains of learning.

When children play, they:

- Test their own theories and adapt them as they go along
- Work through emotional conflicts in creative ways
- Investigate social roles in preparation for family and community activities
- Contribute to language development and a more focused attention span
- Practice interaction and conversation skills with others, adults and peers

The types of play children usually engage in are sensorimotor exploratory play, constructive play, pretend play, and games. During exploratory play, children explore materials with all their senses to see what will happen. Constructive play involves creating something that can remain after the child finishes playing. Pretend play allows children to set up 'what if' situations. They are able to work through emotional conflicts and try out different social situations. When preschool children play games, they usually play cooperatively, rather than competitively. They want to have a good time spinning spinners, hiding, searching, moving pieces, and picking up cards. They are beginning to create their own games with rules.

> **Supporting children's learning through play is a primary goal of the preschool teacher.**

In the classroom, teachers should:

- Value children's play/work time and talk to children about their play
- Play with children and scaffold their learning through play experiences
- Provide a playful atmosphere—a learning environment that encourages lots of playful times
- Encourage children to think about their play/work. What do they want to do? What did they do? How might they do something different next time? What other materials do we need to play this again?

Through play, children grow and develop. They use their small and large muscles and gain mastery over their bodies. They experience and navigate social situations, problem solve, and often cope with conflicting emotions. They interact with other children and with adults. They experiment, explore, imagine, pretend, play-act, dramatize, role-play and more. They succeed, they fail, and they learn.

Active Learning

Active learning is a teaching strategy that places the responsibility of the learning on the learner—even if the learner doesn't realize it. Active learning transforms students from passive listeners to active participants.

Active learning requires that children have *materials* that they can *manipulate* in many ways, that they have choice in how to use them, and that there is *language* (talk) and *support* (scaffolding) from adults as children work and play. These last two elements—language and support—take an active learning approach to the next level engagement. Talking with children about what they are doing and asking questions or providing ideas and materials can help move the child to a higher order of thinking and learning. This approach requires a skilled and trained teacher to facilitate children's learning in an active way.

> **Active Learning is more than hands-on learning. When planning for children, remember to include the five elements of Active Learning in your lesson plans—choice, materials, manipulation, language, and support.**

There will be plentiful opportunities for young children to sit passively at desks in school. The preschool years is not this time. Children in preschool learn about the world through play and exploration—they need to be active participants in their learning. They need to be messy and loud, ask questions and expect responses. They need to tear things apart to see how they work, and put things together with their own two hands.

Consistency

Work to create a habit of consistency in the classroom. Ensure that not only your daily routines and environments are consistent and predictable—so that children know what to expect and what comes next—but also for your day-to-day classroom and behavior "management" techniques. Children often don't respond to rules, but they can understand concepts and expectations.

Teachers have varying preferences of classroom management. Some may prefer children ask questions during Circle Time. Others may want children to sit quietly and listen. The important thing is for all adults in the classroom to keep consistency in mind, and to always do things the same way, every day. If the teacher's expectation is that all children sit "crisscross applesauce" and keep hands in their laps while listening to a story, then be sure to do it the same way, every day. Other teachers may be more comfortable with children sitting however they are comfortable, so that the reading experience for them is fun and pleasurable.

Routines

Daily routines form the basic structure of a preschooler's day. Consistent daily routines help children make sense of their world and maintain order in their lives. Children should be able to predict what will happen next and begin to understand their role in the activities of the day. When routines are predictable, children feel safe and in control of their environment. This comfort level allows them to explore the classroom, take on new challenges a bit at a time, and puts them in a better place to manage change when it occurs. If children's behavior becomes predictably difficult consistently during a certain part of the day, perhaps take a look at that part of the day and determine if there are changes in the routine that need to be made. Is the time segment too long? Are children too tired? Are there too many transitions and children are confused? When behavior issues arise, example your routine to determine if small adjustments may make a difference.

Environment

The design and physical arrangement of the preschool classroom is the starting point for delivering appropriate and engaging learning experiences for young children. When designed with careful thought and planning, the environment can influence how children act and learn. When the classroom is organized and comfortable, and when materials are always found in their correct locations, children can actively engage in the activities provided, and teachers will be able to interact with them productively throughout the day. Again, when behavior issues arise, look to your environment as well, to determine if changes should be made. Are there large, open areas where children are running? Are tall shelves blocking an area creating a hiding spot for children?

Early childhood teachers have long known that the children's preschool environment and the daily routine are two of the most important "teachers" in the classroom. How the classroom environment and the daily routine is set up and created, helps children gain a sense of:

- Predictability
- Belonging
- Security
- Wonder
- Accomplishment.

> **Remember, it's not always what the children do, or don't do, to be successful during their preschool day, but what the adults do to keep the children's days orderly, consistent, and predictable.**

Read more about creating consistent and appropriate learning environments and daily routines for children in the CURRICULUM ELEMENTS section of this curriculum.

The CIRCLES® Curriculum Supports High-Quality Preschool Education

What does high quality preschool education look like? Consider these important elements:

- Parents are always welcome and accommodated in the classroom and are part of the children's day
- Native languages and cultures are recognized and integrated into the curriculum
- The children's daily routine is posted in pictures and words, reading from left to right
- Children are familiar with "what comes next" in the daily routine
- Teaching and learning matches the posted routine and includes a balance of child-directed and teacher-directed experiences—individual, small group, and large group
- Individual cubbies hold children's belongings
- Personal files for each student are available
- Daily lesson plans reflect the experiences happening in the classroom and are connected to learning domains and standards
- Each required segment of the day is included: Circle Time, Small Group Time, Wonder-Work-Share, and Parent and Child Together (PACT) Time®.
- Many books are read to children throughout the day
- Teachers interact with children on the child's level
- Teachers use active learning teaching strategies
- Teachers respect and value children's individual approaches to learning and their learning styles
- Teachers always share the Big Idea (the whole, holistic view) first in terms that children (and parents) can easily grasp and understand
- Teachers allow children time to experiment with materials on their own without supervision
- Teachers allow children time to reflect on their learning before asking questions and expecting responses
- Teachers use self-talk and parallel talk strategies during Small Group and Work Time
- Teachers use open-ended questions when appropriate and avoid quizzing children for quick responses
- Teachers record anecdotal notes while observing children and use them to plan instruction
- Screenings and assessments are conducted and teachers use assessment information to plan instruction
- The classroom environment includes the basic learning areas—House, Block, Art, Book, Writing, and Computer/Technology Areas
- Developmentally and culturally appropriate materials are available—enough for several children to play and interact with together. The materials are open-ended and interesting
- Teamwork—both teachers participate, teach, and support each other
- Teamwork—parents and teachers work together to support the child's academic progress

The CIRCLES® Frameworks

Curriculum: A written plan to support children's learning and development

The pathway to curriculum development in a preschool program is grounded in the curriculum's philosophy and guiding principles. High quality preschool curricula provide an underlying foundation of developmentally appropriate practice regarding classroom environments, daily routines, cultural responsiveness, and family engagement. The written curriculum plan includes the goals for children's development and learning, and the experiences planned by teachers to help children reach these goals. What staff, children, and parents do every day builds the curriculum. The materials, strategies, and resources used by teachers support the implementation of the curriculum.

Curriculum is often regarded as the "what" or the content of learning. We think of curriculum in terms of skills and knowledge, and goals and lesson plans. In our CIRCLES preschool classrooms we take a broader view of curriculum. We focus on the "whole child" and are concerned with supporting all areas of children's learning, growth, and development—which means everything we do, including setting up our learning environment, selecting materials, assessing children's skills, choosing instructional strategies and writing lesson plans, and facilitating interactions with children, is part of our curriculum.

The CIRCLES Curriculum approach is inclusive of families and culture and provides a curriculum model that can adapt to any American Indian preschool program. The curriculum has a proven track record with preschool children who reside in rural, urban, high poverty, and high needs areas to better prepare them for successful kindergarten entry.

The CIRCLES Curriculum consists of three Curriculum Frameworks and seven Curriculum Elements. In this section we will describe the three CIRCLES Curriculum Frameworks.

The **CIRCLES Program Framework** lays the foundational groundwork for teaching and learning. It addresses how the *child learns and is taught* within his or her own *home, school,* and *community*. It takes into consideration children's unique approaches to learning and their preferred learning styles. The foundational framework is the result of evidence-based practices and lessons learned working with American Indian children/families and specifically includes:

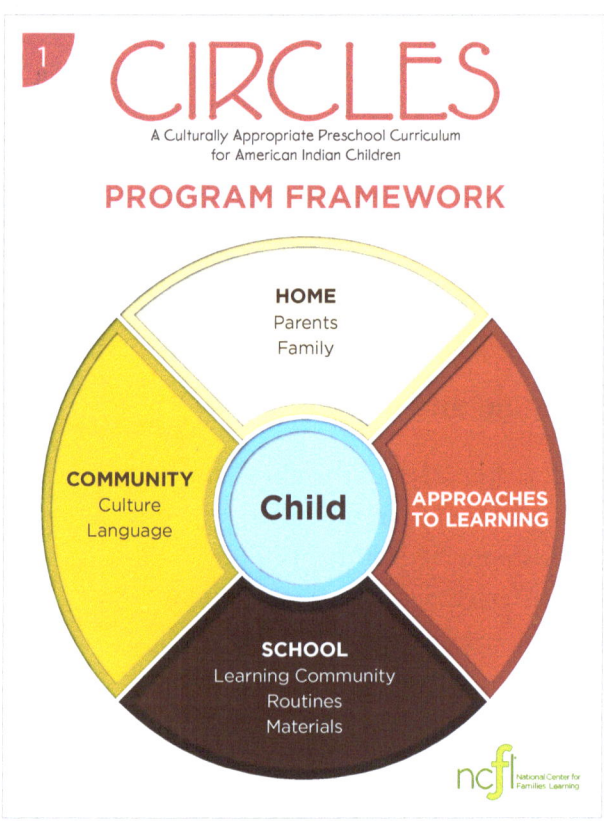

- A balanced approach to preschool that nourishes children's wonder and creativity within an evidence- and standards-based curriculum
- Culturally responsive instruction that addresses the prominent learning styles of American Indian children
- A strong focus on family engagement that impacts academic achievement
- Evidence-based language and literacy practices that support both the child's Native language and skill development in English.

In this foundational framework, we represent children at the center of their learning. We know that children learn best within learning communities that are inclusive of their home culture, their Native language, and their families.

We also know that children thrive and excel in classrooms with predictable routines, plentiful materials, and engaged learning—and with instructional experiences that are guided by standards, evidence-based research, and ongoing monitoring and assessment.

Additionally, we know that children create their own learning experiences, and when they do, they learn best. The CIRCLES Curriculum recognizes that children's approaches to learning are to be nurtured and supported. The specific approaches to learning we will discuss in this curriculum are *wonder and curiosity, initiative and persistence, cooperation, reflection, problem solving and experimentation, engagement and attentiveness,* and *developing habits*. These approaches to learning manifest themselves in all the areas of the CIRCLES Teaching Framework discussed next.

The **CIRCLES Teaching Framework** represents the seven domains of children's learning aligned with common philosophies of Native culture. Those domains of learning are:

- Language and Literacy
- Math
- Science
- Social Studies
- Social-Emotional Development
- Physical Development
- Creative Arts

Teachers develop goals and lesson plans for children from these domains of learning based on what they know about their students, their observation of students, and what they learn about students from ongoing assessment. They then facilitate children's learning throughout the instructional day by adapting classroom routines, materials and strategies to meet children's needs in each domain of learning.

The content areas of the CIRCLES Teaching Framework align with areas of life and learning that are core values of American Indian culture:

- Knowledge and Wisdom
- Communication and Creativity
- Community and Family
- Strength and Introspection

The third framework, the **CIRCLES Learning Framework**, is focused on a specific teaching strategy that helps to not only frame the children's morning routine, but also guide the teacher in how to conduct and structure certain elements—such as Circle Time, Small Group Time, and Wonder-Work-Share time—within the morning routine. This strategy is based on learning styles relevant to American Indian learners and supports children's individual approaches to learning.

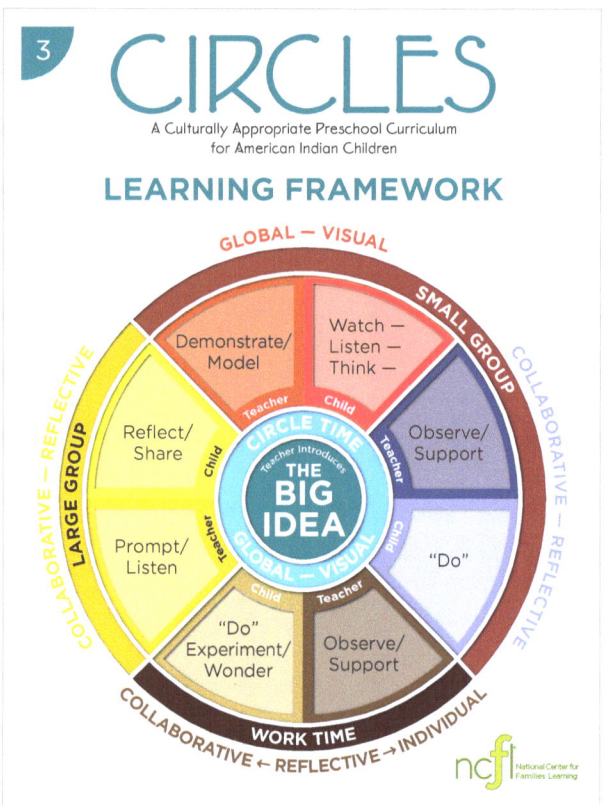

We know that many American Indian children learn best when teachers recognize and support children's individual learning styles, and when teachers use a variety of teaching strategies to address those learning styles throughout the teaching day. Those learning styles include:

- A global "big picture" view of the subject/topic being taught

- Visual models or a demonstration of the task being taught

- Time for reflective learning—times for children to be silent and watchful, to explore and experiment, and to approach the learning in their own way. Times for children to be verbal in their reflection or to silently reflect.

- Times of the day for children to work in collaborative groups, and times for children to work, experiment, and explore alone.

The **CIRCLES Learning Framework** will be discussed in more detail in the following Curriculum Elements sections, *The Teaching Strategy* and *The Morning Routine*.

The CIRCLES Curriculum for American Indian Children

Ideally, American Indian children learn best from American Indian teachers. Many tribal communities, however, do not have certified and available Native teachers—therefore, non-American Indian teachers are often hired. The guidance provided by this curriculum will support the teacher who has limited experience teaching American Indian children, or working or living in Native communities. Of course, all teachers, including those who are American Indian, can benefit from using the strategies and guidance outlined in this curriculum approach. There are many other cultures and ethnic groups that can benefit from teachers recognizing children's individual learning styles and approaches to learning.

This curriculum approach is built by teachers weekly as they consider children's needs, goals, developmental skill levels, and interests learned from observation and assessment; the academic expectations for kindergarten entry; the preschool learning domains; and input from parents. This is an active learning, hands-on, wonder-based approach to instruction, where children imagine, explore, and discover the world around them. CIRCLES is designed to inspire and stimulate the wonder, creativity, and development of young children within the context of a standards-based educational system and within a cultural context.

> **The CIRCLES® Curriculum is built weekly by teachers. The written plan is constructed from the knowledge of where children are *today*, and where teachers want to take children *tomorrow*.**

CIRCLES

1

A Culturally Appropriate Preschool Curriculum
for American Indian Children

PROGRAM FRAMEWORK

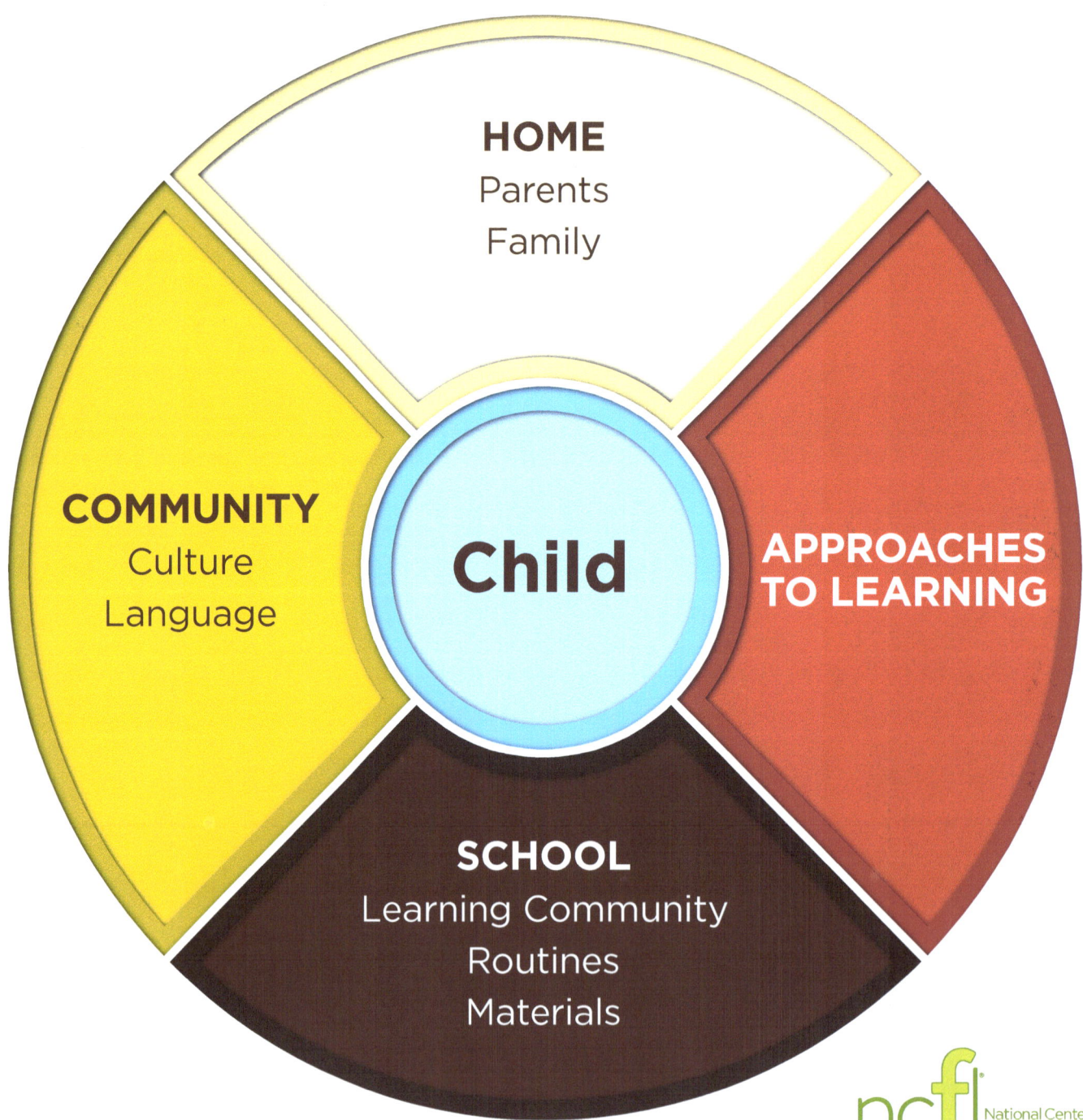

HOME
Parents
Family

COMMUNITY
Culture
Language

Child

APPROACHES TO LEARNING

SCHOOL
Learning Community
Routines
Materials

ncfl National Center for Families Learning

CIRCLES

2

A Culturally Appropriate Preschool Curriculum for American Indian Children

TEACHING FRAMEWORK

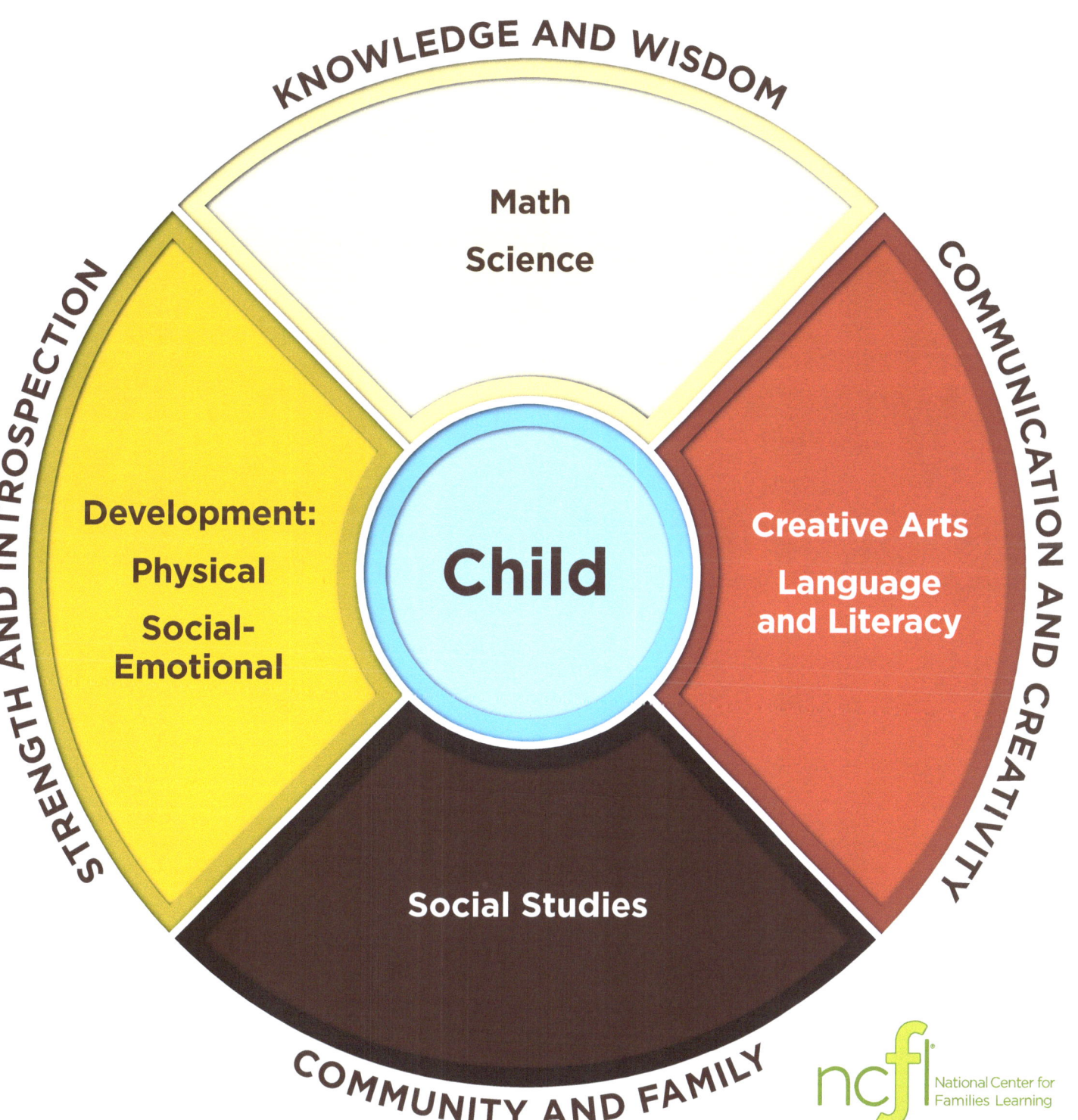

ncfl National Center for Families Learning

CIRCLES

3

A Culturally Appropriate Preschool Curriculum for American Indian Children

LEARNING FRAMEWORK

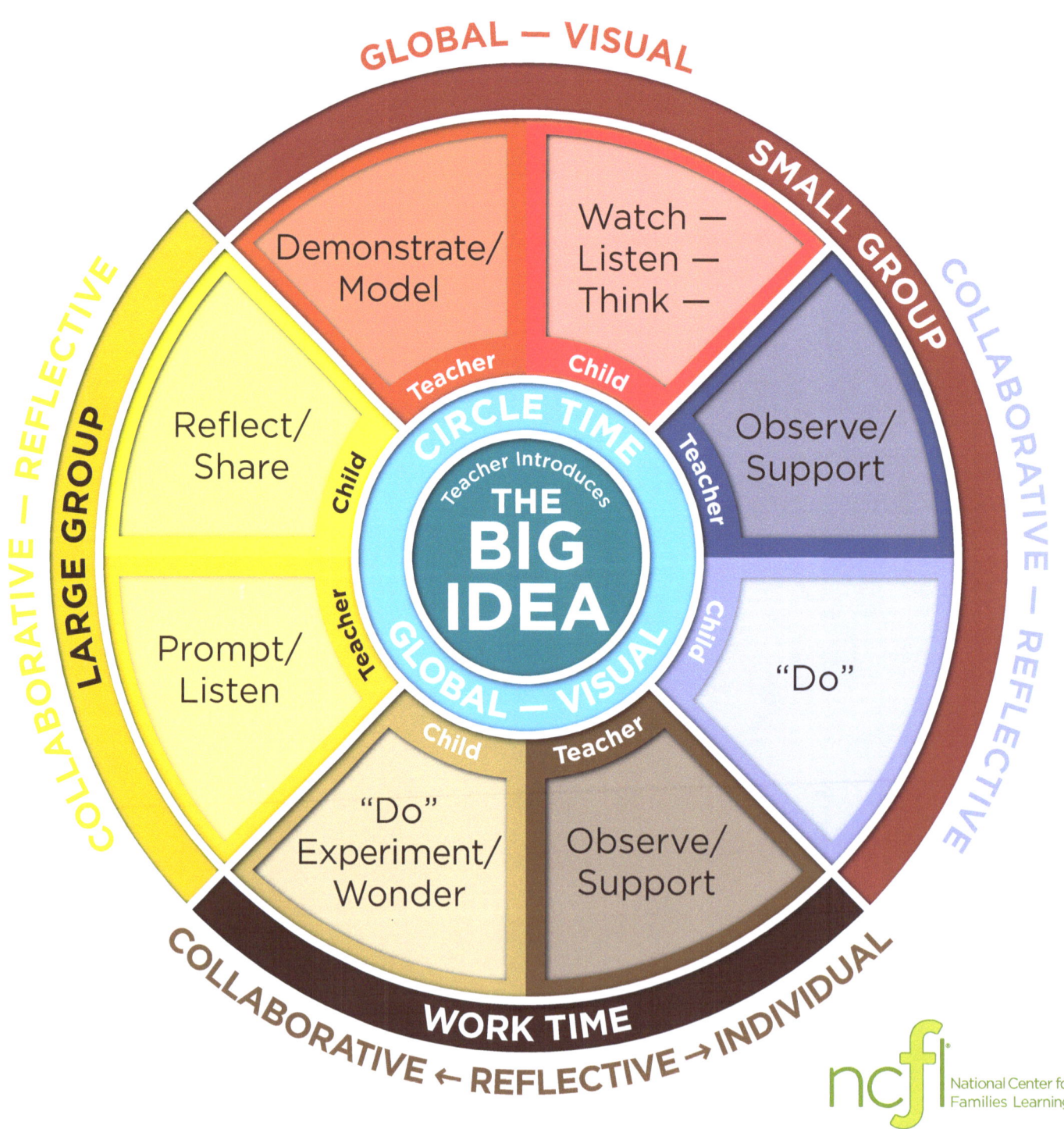

CIRCLES® Curriculum Elements

What are the CIRCLES® Curriculum Elements?

In the CIRCLES Curriculum, the Curriculum Elements are those essential and intentional focuses of learning that happen every day in the classroom. The elements are made up of evidence-based strategies and early childhood best practice. Each individual element can stand on its own—but when all seven are combined collectively in a program, the results are powerful. Together, these seven elements are the core of the CIRCLES Curriculum.

The seven Curriculum Elements are:

1. Culture & Learning Styles
2. The Teaching Strategy
3. The Classroom Environment
4. The Morning Routine
5. Planning for Children
6. Language & Literacy Skill Development
7. Family Engagement

Five of these seven curriculum elements will be discussed in detail in the following chapters. Those elements are Culture and Learning Styles, The Teaching Strategy, The Classroom Environment, The Morning Routine, and Planning for Children.

The Curriculum Elements of Language and Literacy Skill Development and Family Engagement, have their own dedicated supplemental books, which are companion books to this CIRCLES® Core Curriculum book.

The next few chapters will:

1. Define the element
2. Provide a detailed description or scenario of the element
3. Discuss how to implement the element in a preschool classroom and when necessary, provide step-by-step guidance
4. Share specific strategies associated with the element
5. Provide examples of what the element looks like in the classroom

Culture and Learning Styles

What we've learned working with American Indian programs

NCFL has worked with diverse populations and communities within American Indian tribal nations across the United States. From Choctaw, Mississippi to Puyallup, Washington, and many American Indian schools in between, we've learned there are differences, and many similarities, between American Indian schools and communities.

Communities differ depending upon a number of factors, but culture is a part of everyone, and everything. Culture is not a separate concept, but is inherent in every person, school, organization, activity, and conversation. By listening and observing, we come to understand each community, person, and the culture within—with good intentions and without assumptions. This builds trusting relationships. There is a spectrum of how traditional and modern culture is part of each person's life. People can be both traditional and modern, and are often both.

The sense of who American Indian people are and where they came from is grounded in their culture. When adults and children introduce themselves, they often place themselves within their family and community, all of their relations, their place of origin and lineage, and/or their clan. Relationships matter. Many communities are made up of closely related families and often take time to accept outsiders.

Isolated and rural tribal communities tend to be very traditional. Language and culture are not separate but intertwined and interdependent. Native languages, however, may not be the first language of many families—English is often the dominant language. Many tribes are working to revitalize their language and culture by implementing them into their school curricula. We learned that when learning language, it's not just the words, but also the story around the words that are significant. Young children learn their Native language best when they are immersed in it, when teachers and parents speak the language every day, all day. Sometimes teachers benefit from a reminder to use the Native language throughout the day at school, even when they are bilingual.

Rural communities have their own barriers and social issues that are different from those of urban American Indian communities. These barriers can contribute to less learning time and to a lack of access to educational services. Transportation issues can present a barrier for parents' participation in their children's school events—or even to their getting to school at all. Dirt roads can become nonexistent in wind storms and monsoon weather, hampering travel to anywhere. Sometimes school busses have difficulty getting to students, especially in muddy weather in some areas, snow in others. In some very isolated areas, schools may be an hour or more from communities, which means children may ride the school busses for an hour or more one way, and then back home again. This makes for a long day for preschool age children and their parents—something to be considered when planning family learning programs.

Parts of many reservations and communities are still stricken with poverty. Many rural families live with only the necessities and some without running water or electricity. While some view the conditions as "3rd world," tribes often see this lack of dependence of modern conveniences as being self-sufficient. We have learned to be careful of assumption. Other communities are more modern and westernized, and struggle to maintain the traditional culture and language of their ancestors.

In many communities, jobs are scarce, drug and alcohol addiction is prevalent, and domestic violence is an ever-present concern. These barriers often hamper, or create roadblocks, to parent and family engagement with their children's schools. These are some of the social issues that we often must address, and help families overcome, in family education programs.

American Indian parents and families

All parents want the best for their children, and most parents understand the value of education. Families want their children to be ready for school, but also welcome guidance, support, and advice about *how* they can best help their children. Remembering that parents are a child's best first teacher is important for American Indian families—parents are the ones who make the big decisions about their children's education, and how they transmit and encourage language and culture in their families, and in their children's lives.

Parents, however, often tell us they did not have good experiences in school, and therefore are sometimes leery of sending their children, let alone taking part in school activities themselves. They may not talk of school as a positive place and are reluctant to get involved in school activities—as a student or as a parent volunteer. Grandparents may also be uncomfortable, especially if they are non-English speaking. They will often drop off and pick up their grandchildren, but that may be the extent of their involvement.

Because of the expectation for parent and family engagement in the American Indian family literacy programs we have worked with, we learned that parents and grandparents are typically more involved—and that they welcome the invitation to be involved. We'll share those lessons learned of how to engage American Indian parents and families in this chapter.

American Indian preschool children

Like all children, a variety of factors influence whether an American Indian child is ready for school, or not. A child may be curious, excited, and eager for the experience. Or, she or he could be shy, guarded, and unsure. Many factors contribute to a child's readiness.

Evaluation data and general observations from the FACE program tell us many things about the American Indian preschool children we have worked with over the years, such as:

- Most of the preschool children come to school eager to participate and play. Many have never participated in group social settings before and are learning to be social with other children.
- Like many children, they come to school with less face-to-face interaction and lack the personal skills to socialize, initialize play, and to interact with peers. Whether due to more exposure to video games, tablets, and phones, or a lack of parental engagement, the end result is the same—socialization is an important first step, and an ongoing process, in preschool.
- Some children come to school tired. A full day program is a long day for three- and-four-year-old children. They often need significant rest time and flexibility is a must.
- Some children are undernourished. There is a rise of children with obesity and diabetes on American Indian reservations. Most children qualify for free breakfast/lunch under the Federal Lunch Program.
- A large number of American Indian three-year-olds come to preschool with language and speech delays, limited English language, and/or limited Native language skills.
- Many American Indian preschool children come to school with developmental delays, and may not have been previously screened or assessed for delays. FACE programs screen and assess children on an ongoing basis to detect delays and refer children for services.
- Of the children in preschool who require intervention and are referred for services and have an Individualized Education Program (IEP), approximately 25% did not need an IEP at kindergarten entry after attending FACE.
- Some children's families are transient. Children enroll, stay for a couple of months, unroll, and re-enroll in school in a new location. Sometimes in the same location. Because families may struggle financially, they change locations to live with different family members. When this happens, children often do not get the benefit of a consistent school routine.

Preschool is often the first group social experience for American Indian children to interact with other peers their age—and an adjustment period may be required. As with most children entering preschool, learning basic social skills comes gradually. Many American Indian children are not familiar with the abundance of toys and materials they may see at school, and may have to learn how to play cooperatively and share. Some children may be overwhelmed, so it is a good idea to start the beginning of the year off with fewer materials on the shelves.

When English is the first language of American Indian families, children may lack traditional cultural knowledge and the use of their Native language due to non-exposure, or because parents choose to use English at home. In other families and tribes, where the Native language is spoken fluently and often by parents, English is generally not the first language, and children come to preschool learning two languages.

Children's socialization, Native and English language learning, and school readiness are primary concerns for preschool children in American Indian schools.

Start with culture

"Intergenerational transmission of a culture and its knowledge passes from parent to child. During the first years of life, almost everything a child learns depends on experiences the family provides," (Hart & Risely, 1995).

Why start with culture? Culture is everything. It defines how we think, what we learn, and how we see the larger world. It also defines how we speak, worship (or not), the foods we eat, the music we listen to, the books we read, and how we view art. Culture may define our friends and our enemies. It contributes to our behaviors, interactions, the understanding of our immediate world and the larger world around us. So much of our culture is defined by the types of socialization we experience within our families, and in our communities.

Why should we not expect then, that culture would play a huge role in how we learn?

Children use their knowledge of culture to create their own understanding of their world.

Understanding how young American Indian children view their worlds is important for preschool teachers. The literature suggests that "cultural values and early socialization experiences influence the way American Indian children understand their world" (Swisher, 1991).

Young children in preschool are still forming their views and figuring out their worlds—but even though their socialization is still in the formative stages, so much of their family and community culture is already embedded into their young lives. "Children's identity and sense of self are inextricably linked to the language they speak and the culture in which they have been socialized" (Crago, 1988, as cited in California Department of Education, 2008).

Preschool children have a limited viewpoint—and often only that of what they experience with their parents at home, and in their surrounding communities. They also have a lot of experiences ahead of them—including their preschool experiences—to contribute to their views, which makes the preschool teacher's job all the more important. Young children form their views about school around their first experience—which is often preschool.

Preschool teachers have the unique responsibility of creating a classroom learning environment that mimics the family or community culture of the child. Providing experiences and an environment that makes both children and parents feel comfortable, helps children more easily adjust to the new experience of going to school.

Cultural norms may also define how children respond in group situations and among their peers—especially in learning situations. The more rural the community—and perhaps the smaller and more isolated—the more prevalent the traditional cultural norms reflected in those communities. In opposition, urban tribes that are more assimilated into cities and western culture may develop a more modern version of those same cultural norms.

Many American Indian communities value humility and harmony (Swisher, 1991). Because of this, sometimes American Indian children are uncomfortable placing themselves "above" their peers in a learning situation. A child might choose to not respond to a question from a teacher—even though he knows the correct answer—because he doesn't want to appear superior to the other children in the group. This is possibly a learned behavior from parents or family. "In many native societies humility of an individual is to be respected and preserved. Advancing oneself above others or taking oneself too seriously violates this key value" (Swisher, 1991). Other American Indian children may not attempt a response to an unfamiliar question for fear of not performing well (Morgan, 2009).

To avoid setting up this dynamic in the classroom, teachers can modify their teaching strategies to accommodate this value—and we have taken this cultural norm into consideration in how we have designed this curriculum.

Consider learning styles

Similar to cultural norms, learning styles grow out of how a child comes to know and understand his or her world. According to Vygotsky (1986) children learn "how to learn" through socialization—in the same way children acquire their cultural norms.

Before we delve into the learning styles of American Indian children, it is important to understand that we must be careful to never make generalizations, for there is not only one style of learning for all American Indian children. Evidence has identified patterns of learning, but there are significant variations to consider (Pewewardy, 2002). Research does not indicate a unique American Indian way of learning—although paying careful attention *to common differences* between American Indian and mainstream students is important (Morgan, 2009).

American Indian children, like all children, are individuals who differ dramatically from one another, even within their own communities. Over generalizing can lead to stereotypical notions, discriminatory practices, and inappropriate excuses for failure in teaching (Swisher, 1991).

Early childhood best practice says it best. All children—American Indian and non-American Indian children alike—develop similarly, but differently. Children grow and develop within the same processes, but at a different rate or pace of growth. All children have different learning styles and preferences. Good teachers vary their teaching strategies to accommodate all children, and strive to address all children's learning styles, their developmental needs, and their academic goals. To do this, teachers need to know and understand the children in their classrooms. They do this by using ongoing observation, screening and assessment, and by incorporating a variety of teaching strategies. Then they can plan for and teach all children accordingly.

St. Charles and Costantino (2000) determined that American Indian learners typically (1) value and develop acute *visual* discrimination skills in the use of imagery, (2) value *cooperative behavior* and excel in cooperative environments, (3) perceive *globally*, and (4) are *reflective leaners* (Price, Kellam, & Love, 2009). Cornel Pewewardy, as a result of his literature review, draws similar implications for teachers: "A greater number of American Indian/Alaska Native students have definite learning style tendencies such as strength in the *visual* modality and a preference for *global*, *creative*, and *reflective* styles of learning." He adds that "there is a pressing need for teachers to employ culturally responsive teaching techniques" (Pewewardy, 2002).

A study by Dr. Lloyd Elm (cited in Goin, 1999), in which he tested 800 students for left-brained and right-brained learning styles, showed that American Indian students were primarily right-brained learners. Some *right-brained* learning characteristics include: *visual/spatial* relationships, *music*, *artistic/symbolic*, perception of patterns, *holistic*, intuitive, and *whole-to-part* learning. Considering Howard Gardner's Multiple Intelligences theory (1983), *spatial (visual)*, *musical*, interpersonal (*group learning and interaction*), and *kinesthetic* intelligences fall into the right-brained category. Pewewardy (2002) also talks of the perceptual strengths (*visual, auditory, and kinesthetic*) of AI/AN students.

Let's look at some of these common denominators a little more closely.

Visual discrimination. Besides St. Charles and Constantino, and Pewewardy, other studies show that more American Indian students process *visually*, than students from other groups (Hilberg & Tharp, 2002). The more imaginal learners learn better by utilizing their *visual* perception—images, symbols, and diagrams. They also remember better when an image, simile or metaphor is used (More, 1993). American Indian students seem to perform best in classrooms that involve a great deal of visualization (Pewewardy, 2008).

Cooperative learning. Pewewardy (2008) also explains that American Indian students are more likely to prefer working in a group, such as in *cooperative or group learning* situations, rather than in isolation. Students who like to work in groups are also *holistic* thinkers, and perceive things in relation to the *whole* (Morgan, 2009), which can further explain why learning in groups, or cooperative learning, is a preference. This could also be considered a cultural norm, since traditionally at home, many American Indian children learn to collaborate with others (brothers, sisters, and family members) to finish tasks and solve problems.

Global learners. According to More (1993), American Indian students are often *global learners*, who tend to understand best when the overall concept is presented first, which aligns with the *whole-to-part* learning characteristic of a *right-brained* learner. *Global* (*holistic*) learners often require an overall picture first when learning a task. Generally speaking, American Indian students are more *global learners* than their Anglo counterparts (Hilberg & Tharp, 2002).

Reflective learners. American Indian students are more likely to be strong in a reflective learning style. When students learn reflectively, they completely think through their new learning before using it, they take time to respond, and they depend less on external feedback (More, 1993). Some students learn best by observing tasks they are to perform, reflecting on the observation, and then responding or performing. Pewewardy (2008) explains that American Indian students often tend to reflect more than mainstream students—reflective students take more time than others to gather evidence before offering a response (Morgan, 2009).

Reflective learning can have multiple layers, such as the following:

- ***Demonstration and observation.*** To a great extent, learning in traditional American Indian cultures is based on observation and demonstration—because that is the way children are usually taught at home by their parents or elders (Red Horse, 1980; Pewewardy, 2008). When a parent models a skill for a child, children watch, listen, and then probably think about what they have learned. More (1989) describes this kind of learning as "watch then do."

- ***Watch then do. Listen then do. Think then do.*** American Indian children seem to learn better when taught as their parents teach them. This modeling is generally expected to be done with respective listening and attention, which means no questions or discussion while the elder is "teaching." They watch and listen, then think, and finally do.

- ***Reflective learning*** can have multiple layers. American Indian children seem to learn best by observing a demonstration (or a modeling) of a task, listening intently without questioning or asking questions, thinking about the task and how it was done, and then experimenting with the task on their own, or collaboratively, until they are ready to perform.

In Summary

This curriculum—***CIRCLES: A Culturally Appropriate Preschool Curriculum for American Indian Children***—is based on the knowledge gained from 25 years of working in the field of early childhood education in American Indian preschools, plus the knowledge gained from the evidence that shows us how American Indian children learn best.

Our goal is to provide a unique and appropriate preschool curriculum that helps both American Indian, and non-American Indian teachers of American Indian preschool children, create developmentally and culturally appropriate learning environments, daily routines, and learning experiences for American Indian preschoolers. The ultimate goal then, is to prepare these young children in the best way possible for school and life experiences.

Learning styles of American Indian children vary, but there are patterns of learning styles that fit best for many American Indian children. Those prominent learning styles include,

- *A global or holistic style*—for the organization of information
- *A visual style*—for mentally representing information
- *A reflective style*—for processing information, and
- *A collaborative approach*—for completing tasks (Hillberg & Tharp, 2002).

Culture In the Classroom

There is no one-way to infuse culture into an American Indian classroom learning environment or a preschool curriculum. Culture is woven throughout the room, the day, the lesson plans, and the interactions among the children and adults in the classroom. It's not an add-on—it is what *is*, every single day. Culture *is* the curriculum, *is* the learning environment, and *are* the interactions that happen.

In the previous section, we provided an overview of what we've learned about American Indian culture in schools and communities, along with a review of the literature about how American Indian children learn. In this brief section on Culture, we provide an overview of basic principles to consider when working with American Indian children and families, and some over-arching guidance for implementing culture into every day practice.

We don't stop there, however. Within this curriculum, you will see culture infused into all facets and layers. After all, culture is the curriculum.

Unique tribes and communities = unique cultures

As we have already established, cultural differences exist from tribe to tribe, from rural to urban communities, from economic to educational levels, and from English to Native speakers. American Indian schools often have their own unique culture, within their own unique community and tribe, and focus best on the cultural lives that children and parents live every day—within their home, their community, and their tribe.

Language issues differ from school to school, from tribe to tribe. Some young American Indian preschoolers come to school understanding or using very few English language words. Often these children live within a rural and possibly isolated communities where the Native language is dominant and spoken in the home—as opposed to areas where the Native language is no longer spoken, and where children come to school with a higher level of English language skills.

Each situation has unique needs for teachers to address. Preschoolers who are Native speakers with spotty or non-existent English language skills, will need to work to catch up with their peers to speak fluent English before kindergarten. Knowing and being able to speak both languages as they grow up, will be beneficial to them in the long run. Preschoolers who speak only English will benefit from language preservation and cultural strategies embedded into the preschool curriculum. The bottom line is, the needs of all the children in the classroom, no matter where they come to school on the English/Native language continuum, require attention.

Teaching culture

Many American Indian schools are fortunate to have designated culture teachers within their schools who can provide cultural guidance to teachers, and help to infuse culture into all classrooms. This support can range from providing experiences and lessons to sustaining and preserving the Native language, to sharing oral history, songs, dance and stories, and to learning about traditional ways of living.

When American Indian teachers are in the classroom, attention to culture often comes naturally. It is part of their everyday life. Native languages, such as Navajo or Choctaw, may be spoken throughout the day, or spoken interchangeably with English. There are times, however, when preschool classrooms in American Indian schools have teachers who are not American Indian, and who do not speak the language. It is more difficult for non-Native teachers to interject appropriate culture and language experiences, or to teach with strategies that best support Indian children, without the help of others. The most logical people to rely on for guidance and assistance, is the preschool co-teacher (who most frequently will be American Indian), the school culture teacher, the parents of the children in the classroom, and the elders in the community.

Talk with children, parents, and elders

Remember, building culture in the classroom is part of building the learning community. A good place to start is by talking with children and parents. What is important to them? What does the community look like, and what do the people who live there like to do? What are their jobs? Include those kinds of things in the classroom. For example, if rodeo is a big event that both children and parents talk about frequently, then build rodeo into the classroom (a saddle and boots in the House Area; books about rodeo and ranches in the Book Area; an 8-second clock in the Block area; rodeo-type activities in gross motor play). Ask parents what is important to them—what would they like to see in the children's classroom to represent who they are? More family pictures? Real cultural items? (baskets, clothing, musical instruments, fishing gear, etc.) More Native books in the classroom to represent their tribe? Native music and dance? Parents can provide wonderful insight into how they see the cultural aspect of the classroom community—what's missing and what's needed.

One caution when placing real cultural items in the classroom—be sure to check with parents, the culture teacher, or elders if appropriate, as to the suitability of doing so. Some items are sacred and not to be treated as a child's plaything. In some tribal cultures, playing with a drum, or dressing up in ceremonial or traditional clothing, may be accepted. In others, it may not be permitted. The rule of thumb if you are not familiar with the culture of the community, is to respectfully ask first.

Some ideas for teachers—beginning guidance

The following list may provide some initial guidance for preschool teachers to infuse culture and language into their preschool learning community:

- If the Native language is a spoken language, speak it all day long with the children, along with English words. It is important for children to hear the sounds and words of both languages.
- Consult with families, community members, and elders, as permitted and appropriate, to include culture and language in the curriculum.
- Label important areas and items in the classroom with the Native word for the object first, the English word second.
- Sing traditional songs and tell stories; read traditional Native books of the children's tribe and others. Work with children to count, learn colors, and other concepts words in their Native language.
- Incorporate items from the culture (as appropriate) or the community into the classroom learning environment. For example: fishing gear, canoes, woven baskets or rugs, jewelry or clothing for dress-up, pictures of children's families, Native posters and sayings, and so much more. Every community is different and therefore every classroom will be different.
- Connect with the school's culture teacher and other outside resources to enhance the early childhood curriculum.
- Connect curriculum and standards to culture—for example, Science to farming or harvest, fishing, gardening; Creative Arts to dance, jewelry or rug making; traditional storytelling to Language and Literacy Development; Math to counting beads, patterns, etc.

Remember, the suggestions made here are beginning guidelines for considering how to best approach culture in a preschool program. As always, the local school, community, and tribe define how culture and language is best taught in their own communities.

Checklist for a Family and Culture Rich Preschool Environment

*Check the items you do well and put a * beside items you want to implement*

_____ Books in the classroom reflect families, their cultures and the community.

_____ Display space in the classroom is provided for children's and parents' input.

_____ Frequent opportunities are provided for parents to read to their children, or small groups of children.

_____ The Book Area (and other areas of the classroom) has comfortable seating space for parents.

_____ The school or community library is often used and families are encouraged to check out books.

_____ Children and parents tell family stories and make up their own stories.

_____ Children and parents' home languages are valued in the classroom.

_____ Oral tradition and storytelling is encouraged by inviting grandparents or community elders into the classroom to share stories in their home languages or in English.

_____ Materials and equipment in the classroom reflects the cultures of the families, their community, and their own homes.

_____ Posted information in the classroom is at the eye level of the intended audience (children or parents).

_____ Opportunities are provided for children to listen to books on tape recorded by parents or other family members, in their home language or in English.

_____ Parents are welcome contributors of ideas and help plan activities for children.

_____ Teachers know children's and families' home backgrounds, interests and cultures and consider these when planning for children.

_____ Teachers consider parents, caregivers and family members an extended part of their teaching team and the learning community.

_____ Families and community members are invited into the classroom to talk about their work.

_____ All languages of the community are valued, honored, and spoken in the classroom (if language is spoken).

_____ Cultural events and holidays are respected in the classroom.

_____ Books and other literacy materials are routinely provided to families for use in the home environment.

_____ Accommodations are made for communicating with parents with special needs, e.g., low literacy skills, or non-English speakers.

The Teaching Strategies

The CIRCLES® Curriculum supports the various learning styles of American Indian children. The basics of the curriculum are grounded in evidence-based principles and focused on the grounding tenets of early childhood best practice. In the CIRCLES Curriculum, planning for children is built around these important strategies

- The Big Idea
- The CIRCLES Teaching Strategy
- Active Learning
- Parallel and Self Talk

The Big Idea is a conversational starting point to share with children and parents. It is the one specific topic that flows through the children's morning routine and is reflected on the daily lesson plan.

Deciding on The Big Idea: Think of The Big Idea as your one point of focus for children and parents—a common theme that will run through your Circle Time, Small Group Time, and into Work Time. *This doesn't mean that the Big Idea is the only thing you teach that day, but it's one idea or topic you want to draw children's attention to throughout the morning routine.* [More about The Morning Routine in the next chapter.] Children will still be exposed to other Learning Domains throughout the day, within the learning environment, at Work Time, PACT Time, and in their afternoon activities.

> The Big Idea is a conversational starting point to share with children and parents. It is directly connected to a CIRCLES® Learning Domain.

<u>Hint:</u> Narrow your focus to a topic manageable for children and parents. This topic is not going to include everything you are teaching (or focusing on) that day, but it is the one "Big Idea" you want to children and parents to connect with that day.

For example, instead of having a Big Idea using big teacher words like, "Today children we are going to "match, sort, and group, and classify items according to one or two attributes," it would be better to simplify that Big Idea and say to children, "Today we are working on matching."

The Big Idea is directly connected to a CIRCLES Learning Domain [see the section, Planning for Children] and should come from observations teachers have made of the children, their interests and next steps, parent input, and screening/assessment data.

The CIRCLES Teaching Strategy

This process can be big, lasting over an entire morning routine, or much smaller, as in one-to-one instruction with a child. It works well for Small Group Time, as well as for planning out the entire day.

1. **The Big Idea.** Share the big idea of what you are teaching and what you want children to learn. Provide children with the *global view*—or the Big Idea—first. Say it in words that children can easily understand.

2. **Model/Demonstrate.** "Do" what you want children to do. Provide a brief demonstration or model. Avoid asking questions at this time, and don't expect many questions from students. Simply do, and talk about what you are doing. Use self-talk and the watch-then-do strategies.

While the teacher is doing, the children…

3. **Observe/Listen.** Children observe and respectfully listen while the teacher is "doing."

4. **Children Do.** Now, children "do" under supervision and teacher observation. Talk about what children are doing (use the parallel talk strategy) and encourage discussion if children want. If children do not want to discuss, that is okay. They could be processing, thinking, and reflecting.

5. **Individual Experimentation.** Continue time for children to experiment with materials without adult supervision. Later, adults can add support as children are more comfortable with the materials. Children need time for trial, error, experimentation and exploration.

6. **Reflection.** Provide time and space for children to reflect on their own or with small or large groups of children. Remember that children reflect in various ways and not all ways are verbal. Use a variety of reflection strategies.

**What teachers do.
What children do.**

1. *Teacher:* **Demonstrate/Model**
2. *Children:* **Watch-then-do**
3. **While children do:** *Teacher* **observes/supports**
4. *Children* **experiment and explore, work on their own**
5. *Teacher* **listens and observes, supports and prompts when appropriate**
6. *Children* **reflect/share (verbal and non-verbal**

What Teachers Do	What Children Do	Learning Style
Demonstrate or model	Watch (listen, think) …	Provide a global/holistic view A visual model
Observe and support (but does not hover or guide); Listen and prompt occasionally; affirm learning.	…then do. Use trial and error, experimentation and exploration	Individual or collaborative work Reflective learning

The CIRCLES Teaching Strategy works well for:

- Small Group Time activities
- Large group activities (Circle Time)
- Individual activities (during Work Time)
- Larger segments of time, such as the Morning Routine (Circle Time, Small Group Time, and Wonder-Work-Share)

There is more information in The Morning Routine chapter of this curriculum about how to use the CIRCLES Teaching Strategy for a large block of time.

Active Learning

Active learning is a teaching strategy that places the responsibility of the learning on the learner—even if the learner doesn't realize it. Active learning transforms students from passive listeners to active participants.

Active learning requires that children have *materials* that they can *manipulate* in many ways, that they have *choice* in how to use them, and that there is *language* (talk) and *support* (scaffolding) from adults as children work and play. These last two elements—language and support—take an active learning approach to the next level engagement. Talking with children about what they are doing and asking questions or providing ideas and materials can help move the child to a higher order of thinking

> **Active learning is more than hands-on learning or "learning by doing." When planning experiences for preschool children, remember to include the five elements of active learning in your lesson plans—choice, materials, manipulation, language, and support from adults.**

and learning. This approach requires a skilled and trained teacher to facilitate children's learning in an active way.

There will be plentiful opportunities for young children to sit passively at desks in school. The preschool years is not this time. Children in preschool learn about the world through play and exploration—they need to be active participants in their learning. They need to be messy and loud, ask questions and expect responses. They need to tear things apart to see how they work, and put things together with their own two hands.

In order to facilitate active learning, teachers should understand that:

- ***Choice supports independent learning.*** When children make their own plans, select the materials they want to use, and carry out their own activities, they feel the power in their own learning. They decide what to do with the materials they select, and guide their own learning around how they use them. They are following their own exploratory path, and not the path of the teacher.

- ***Manipulating materials supports learning.*** Children should have the opportunity to choose from a variety of interesting materials that are easily accessible. Materials are not accessible when they have to ask for them, or when materials or equipment are blocked off (a learning center is closed) or not turned on (computers are in the room but not on). Children should be able to choose from a variety of real and functional everyday objects, found and natural materials, as well as commercially made materials.

    Children manipulate materials using all of their senses. They are free to handle, explore and work with the materials, any way they see fit. They transform and combine materials, using tools and equipment located throughout the classroom, and discover their relationships through direct experience. When children manipulate and experiment with materials, they may be verbal or silent in their work. Children process their learning differently—some like to talk about the process, and others prefer to think and reflect, before speaking.

- ***Talking and listening is part of the learning process.*** Children communicate verbally and non verbally about what they have done, what they are doing, and what they will do. Adults add to the conversation. Sometimes children plan and may set goals (I'm going to make a big tower today) and share that goal with the teacher and other children. Other times they may thoughtfully reflect and think about what they are doing. They may express their observations and feelings along the way (I'm too short to put up the last block!) and problem-solve with others (Can we use that stool to can get higher?). They sometimes ask questions and respond, taking turns in conversation with adults and other children.

- ***Adults support children and add to their learning.*** Adults encourage the children's efforts and help them extend or build upon their work by providing materials and space, observing and listening, talking with them about what they are doing, joining in their play, and helping them learn to solve problems. Adults provide three types of support:
    o Environmental—providing adequate materials and space for using them

- o   Nonverbal—watching and listening to children, nodding, smiling, kneeling, offering new and additional materials
- o   Verbal—conversing with children, referring children to one another, asking questions, responding to questions, adding new words and ideas

Parallel Talk and Self Talk

Parallel talk and self talk are two strategies teachers can use during their morning routine to help children develop their oral language skills and increase vocabulary. The strategies are simple to use and are very effective to use during Small Group Time.

Parallel Talk—When using parallel talk, adults describe the actions of children. "You're playing with the red truck. You're pushing the red truck down the road." This strategy provides children with the words or labels to describe what he/she is doing.

Self Talk—When using self talk, adults describe their own actions. "I'm pouring the apple juice into your yellow cup." By labeling or providing words for your actions, children learn the meanings of words and phrases.

The Classroom Environment

Imagine visiting a preschool classroom anywhere in the world. How do you know when you walk in the door if a classroom is set up appropriately, or if the interactions and learnings inside are consistent with how young children learn? When you step inside the preschool classroom doors, and glance about at the learning environment, can you very quickly respond to these questions:

- What tells me this classroom is for preschoolers?
- What tells me this classroom has extended an open invitation to parents?
- What tells me this classroom is located in an American Indian school?
- What tells me this classroom is located in an American Indian school in this particular American Indian community?

There should be some very concrete clues to help you respond to each of these four questions. When you visit or observe any preschool classroom, you should quickly be able to identify if the classroom is for preschoolers, that parents are involved, and the community where the classroom is located. In this chapter, we will discuss these elements and more.

Preschool teachers have the unique responsibility of creating a classroom learning environment that mimics the family or community culture of the child. Providing experiences and an environment that makes both children and parents feel comfortable, helps children adjust more easily to the new experience of going to school.

> Along with choosing developmentally appropriate materials and creating a safe *learning environment* and predicable *daily routine*, how children and adults *build community* is essential for creating a high-quality preschool classroom experience.

Creating a high-quality preschool classroom environment in any culture involves so much more than knowing how to arrange the furniture, or the kinds of materials to put on the shelves. While materials and room arrangement are critically important, and define a preschool classroom, we also need to consider the interactions that happen inside the four walls of the classroom that create and sustain a climate of building community.

This section on creating a high-quality preschool classroom environment will address the following three topics:

- Building Community
  - Culture
  - Family
  - Interactions
- Room Arrangement
- Choosing Materials

Building Community

Creating an atmosphere of caring and security is a primary goal for preschool. One way is to build community.

Building community within the walls of the classroom helps children and parents feel safe. After all, many parents are leaving their children alone for the day, perhaps for the first time with other adults in the supervision role. Both children and their parents need to feel comfortable. Building community in the classroom goes hand in hand with building trust.

> **Building community in the preschool classroom helps create a sense of predictability, belonging, and security for children.**

Many American Indian tribal communities are close-knit and dependent upon each other. Children and families thrive well in these kinds of supportive communities. Building the learning community within your classroom in a similar way—where children know and trust and respect each other, and the adults/teachers in the classroom—goes a long way toward helping children and their parents feel comfortable at school.

Preschool is a social time as much as it is a learning time. In fact, much of the learning that happens in preschool revolves around children being social. When they are social, children talk, work, play, and solve problems together. They learn where to locate materials, how the classroom works, how the day is structured, and how to interact with others and the elements of the day.

Establishing community is as basic as establishing simple routines, and helping children understand how those routines flow within the classroom environment. The goal is to create a sense of *predictability, belonging,* and *security* for children, and for parents so that they feel comfortable with their child being in the school.

This brand new world of preschool is a challenging experience for many young three- and four-year-olds. For many, this may be the first time to spend their days, or part of their day, in a group, social situation. Remember that for many American Indian children, the preschool experience may be their first real group experience with peers of their age. Therefore, taking care to build the learning atmosphere in the classroom is essential for building positive experiences.

Establishing expectations for children can be as simple as creating a few regular habits to help ground students in their day. Here are a few ideas for helping children understand how the classroom works:

- *Cues and signals* help children remember the sequence and order of the day. Choose basic cues/signals for a few important ideas. Perhaps a hand in the air means everyone stops what they are doing. A familiar song signals clean up time. Dimming the lights means it is time to prepare for rest.
- *A place for everything (and everything in its place)* is a wise, age-old mantra, and a good one. Clearly label shelves in the environment with pictures or objects so that children know on which shelf toys belong.
- *Be consistent.* Whatever routines you establish, always do them in the same way, every day, and have the same daily expectations for children. Preschool-age children's brains are hard-wired to learn with repetition. While doing things at the same time and in the same way every day may seem boring to you, it is a learning experience for children.

Children thrive within a classroom community that provides them with a sense of belonging. Create an inclusive, welcoming environment that supports children and their families.

- *Greet children* at the door every day, say their names, and welcome them into the room. At the end of the day, send them off with a warm good-bye until next time.
- *Identify each child's cubby and/or chair* with her picture and name, so that it clearly identifies the child's space. Having a space of her own within the classroom means "I belong here."
- *Place family pictures in the classroom.* Perhaps have a bulletin board for family events, or for children sharing. Frame snapshots of children and their families, and place them in various areas of the classroom.

Feeling secure within a new environment makes learning so much better. Children feel free to explore and experience new things when they feel safe and secure, and when their ideas are accepted and important.

- *Help children to understand the expectations of arrival and departure times.* Whether they arrive with a parent, or ride a school bus, these beginning and end of day transitions, in and out of school, can sometimes be frightening. Assure children that they don't have to navigate these scary times alone.
- *Post the daily routine schedule on the wall* in such a way that children can "read" and understand what comes next. Simple left-to-right blocks of cards with a picture that represents the element of the schedule is all you need for children at the beginning of the year. Later on, you can add more detail, if you feel children need that. Remember, this posted schedule is for children, not adults, so should be at their eye level. When children

get antsy about when Mom or Granny is coming to pick them up, use the schedule as a tool to help them understand. "In three pictures your Mommy will be here."

- ***Knowing that snacks and meals will arrive on time,*** and at the same time every day, is comforting to children.
- ***Children feel safe and at ease when their personal needs are met.*** Knowing they can use the restroom at will, or get a drink of water when needed, not only encourages independence, but contributes to their comfort level in the classroom. When children are comfortable, they feel freer to explore and learn.
- ***When children speak, offer ideas, and share solutions*** to a problem, always listen respectfully and respond appropriately—and allow children to reflect and respond in their own time, and in their own way.

As communities grow and develop, comfort levels increase. The sense of predictability, belonging, and security are well established a few weeks into the school year, but there are still many things teachers can do to maintain that level of comfort for children.

Personalize your greetings and your good-byes with children. Having a special high-five for one child and sharing a personal observation with another, makes those arrival and departure times special for the child—and often for the parent, too. This intentionality and personalization becomes a part of everything you do and helps children develop a sense of familiarity.

Learning communities for children can extend beyond the classroom to include their families, other children in the school, and community members.

The essential elements of building community include:
- Culture
- Adult/Child Interactions
- Teamwork
- Parent Engagement

Let's take a look into each.

Building Community—*Culture*

The culture of the children in the classroom guides how you create community. Culture is the heart of any community. Teachers in American Indian preschool programs infuse culture and language into most all aspects of the child's day. Strategies can vary from program to program, and tribe to tribe, in order to be culturally relevant. When teachers make the effort to speak the words children know, talk about things children are familiar with, or share in experiences of the community with children and their families—they are saying that what is important to children, also is important to them.

We know that all children learn best when they feel safe and secure, when their physical needs are met, and when they feel their ideas are valued. American Indian children also feel safe, valued, and part of a community when teachers consider the cultural responsiveness of their:

- Classroom environments
- Daily routines
- Teaching strategies
- Interactions with children
- Planning and assessment processes

Here are some ideas for creating a preschool environment that is culturally relevant to the American Indian community:

- Greet children every day with greetings spoken in their Native language.
- Post pictures of families and children in the classroom, along with pictures/posters of American Indian people, subjects, or sayings on the walls.
- Label important items in the classroom in the language of the children first, and English second.
- Provide books in the classroom that reflect the families who live in the community and their cultures. Read books about American Indian families, cultures, traditions, and legend frequently to children.
- Provide frequent opportunities for parents to read to their children, or to small groups of children. Make sure the classroom has comfortable seating for parents or grandparents.
- Respect the home language of the children and families, and speak the Native language throughout the day.
- Encourage oral tradition and storytelling by parents and elders from the community. Invite grandparents or community elders to share stories in their Native languages or in English.

- Provide materials that reflect the culture and communities of the families.
- Create a culture area or add cultural items to various work areas in the classroom.
- Create learning areas to reflect the culture—for example, the House Area could be a Navajo hogan, or an Ojibwa fishing campsite, with tents and poles.
- Create recorded books for children. Provide opportunities for children to listen to books recorded by parents, or elders in the community, that are read in the Native language.

Building Community—*Adult/Child Interactions*

Responsive interpersonal relationships nurture young children's dispositions to learn and impacts their emerging abilities. Social competence and school achievement are influenced by the quality of early teacher-child relationships and by teachers' attentiveness to how the child approaches learning (Bowman, Donovan and Burns, 2001 p.7).

When working with young children, some best practices exist to increase the level of interaction that happens between children and adults. Use these practices to build and support teacher-child relationships:

- *Child's Level.* Interacting at a child's level allows adults to have eye contact with the child and gain the child's full attention. This encourages verbal interaction and prevents the child from feeling he is being overpowered by an adult standing over him.
- *Respond when children initiate communication.* Children are motivated to communicate when adults respond appropriately and promptly to their communication efforts.
- *Respond to non-verbal cues and gestures.* Adults respond to children's spontaneous cues and gestures when communicating by pointing, looking and using words.
- *Conversational turn taking.* Adults participate in authentic conversations with children when they wait for a response from the child before adding additional verbal information.
- *Open-ended questions.* Adults use open-ended questions to stimulate children's talk and thinking. Remember to ask questions children cannot answer with a "yes" or "no" or another one-word answer. Ask questions you do not know the answer to.
- *Parallel talk.* As adult and children work and play together, adults describe the children's actions. For example, with a particularly non-verbal child, the teacher may comment, "You're playing with the red truck." This provides the child with words to describe what he is doing.
- *Self talk.* Adults describe their own actions. "I'm pouring your apple juice into your yellow cup."
- *Use the child's words.* Adults repeat what the child says in the child's words. This not only acknowledges that the child's words are important, but allows the child to hear his own words spoken again.
- *Use silence, observation, understanding and listening.* When entering children's play, adults use this supportive approach before interacting with children. Before offering guidance or suggestions for their play, be silent and observe, understand what they children are doing, and listen for more information. Do you need to interfere and/or support, or are children learning more by working things out on their own.

Building Community—*Teamwork*

In the preschool classroom, the teacher and co-teacher (or assistant teacher in some programs) work together as a team to design and deliver an appropriate educational experience for their students. In a classroom full of three- and four-year-old children, it takes a strong and collaborative team to successfully manage the day and meet the wide range of student needs. It's important in the initial hiring process to ensure that candidates for the teacher and co-teacher positions are committed to the value of teamwork and willing to do what it takes to be part of a functioning and effective teaching team.

In the FACE program, the teacher and co-teacher have always been considered true partners in the teaching process. In other programs, this may not necessarily be the case. However, we highly recommend that the teacher/co-teacher relationship be forged as a team with shared teaching responsibilities. The co-teacher is not the person to always clean up, take children to the restroom, or run errands. The co-teacher assists with Circle Time by sitting in the circle with the children and supporting them—and sometimes leading Circle Time, while the teacher supports the children. The co-teacher may lead other large group activities and conduct Small Group Time. The important element here is for the teacher and co-teacher to discuss and plan responsibilities ahead of time.

As mentioned in an earlier chapter, in many American Indian preschool programs, the co-teachers are often American Indian and from the community. The teacher, however, may be a non-American Indian staff member. In this case the co-teacher should take the lead on culture and language, with the teacher learning and supporting.

Classroom operations will be most effective when the teacher and co-teacher agree on a common approach to arranging the classroom, setting the daily routine, and providing instruction to children. Team members must plan and work together, recognize each other's strengths and talents, and encourage and respect individuality.

Before the start of the school year, the teacher and co-teacher must engage in extensive planning to address questions and make decisions that will affect the daily operation of the classroom. Being "on the same page" will be important so that children and parents hear consistent messages about the preschool program. For example, the team will have to decide:

- How will the classroom be arranged and why? How will our classroom reflect the culture, families and community of the children who are enrolled?
- What materials do we want to include in the classroom, and how do they address the standards?
- What do we know and believe about child development, play and active learning, and how will those ideas influence the way we operate our classroom?
- What will our daily routine look like? What roles do we each have in the segments of the preschool day?
- Within our daily schedule, what routines will we need to establish for children to ensure the smooth and safe operation of the program? For example, hand washing, mealtimes, restroom breaks, moving within the school, arrival and departure procedures, etc.

- What assessments will need to be administered and who will be responsible? When and where will the assessments be given? How will assessment results be used to guide our lesson planning?
- When will we meet each week for lesson planning?
- When will we talk each day about how the day went, any observations we made of children and what might need to be adjusted for tomorrow?
- What approach will we use for guiding children's behavior? How will we communicate our expectations to children and parents? What kind of language will we use to encourage children's efforts? How will we manage behavioral consequences when necessary?
- How will we communicate with each other openly and actively seek to build and maintain a positive working relationship? How will we solve problems as they arise?
- Are there areas of responsibility or instructional topics in the early childhood program around which we need training or additional information? How can we go about obtaining needed resources?
- How will we communicate with the rest of our team, parents/family members, administrators and the school community?

Clearly, team members must choose to be collaborative every day and must view their colleagues as individuals with valuable strengths to offer children and families. Both preschool team members should be familiar with assessment and documentation requirements and must be willing to assign responsibilities in a fair, equitable way. Both should be accountable for knowing the strengths and needs of the children in the class and how to plan lessons and interactions appropriately to build their developmental and academic skills.

In a well-functioning team, members will share responsibilities, respect and support each other, and will teach and learn from each other as they build their understanding of their students, the curriculum, and the ways they can best support families in the program.

Building Community—*Parents*

Parents and teachers alike share a great responsibility in the education of all children. This responsibility lies in the creation of environments, routines, and relationships at home and at school that are responsive to children's needs. Together, parents, teachers and children can form unique partnerships that benefit children's overall academic achievement.

When parents and teachers work together, children benefit. Sometimes parents are unsure of how to support their children's learning. They may not feel comfortable at school. Often, they may not understand the value of positive parent-teacher relationships, nor do they understand how important they are for supporting their children's growth and development. Parents want the best for their children, and their intentions are good. They just might not know what to do.

Research tells us of the added value of positive, shared relationships between parents and teachers. Children, families, and schools benefit when everyone works together.

Parents are the greatest influence on their children's development.

Children grow and thrive within the context of close and dependable relationships, love and nurturance, security, responsive interaction, and encouragement for exploration (Shonkoff & Phillips, 2000). Teachers, classrooms, and schools may change, but parents are a steady influence. When schools provide support for parents and children to interact, children flourish. When schools provide opportunities for parents to get new information, learn, and practice new skills, parents become confident about their parenting.

Parent and family involvement help children transition to kindergarten and elementary school.

Schools that have included parent/family involvement activities have shown positive results in helping children transition to kindergarten and succeed during the primary grades. When parents begin a pattern of involvement in preschool and early care programs, that involvement prepares them for later engagement in kindergarten and elementary school.

Parents help children build relationships with other adults, such as teachers.

Children's relationships with adults form their pathways in school. According to Pianta (1999) "adult-child relationships are critical regulators of development; they form and shape it." Parent-child relationships form the basis for children's learning, development, relationships, and academic achievement. These relationships thrive within children's everyday routines and experiences at home and at school. As parents, teachers, and children form this unique partnership, children begin to experience success.

When parents and teachers are partners, children succeed in school.

According to Epstein and Salinas (2004), a school learning community welcomes all families, regardless of cultural or socio-economic background. All parents want their children to succeed, and all children do better in school when parents and teachers work together as partners to support children's learning.

The Room Arrangement

When Teacher Sarah crosses the threshold to her preschool classroom every morning, she turns on the lights and glances about the room. She always arrives early to make sure the classroom is prepared and ready for her three- and four-year-old children.

The first thing she does is remove the chairs from the tops of the tables, where she had placed them the evening before so the custodian could run the vacuum. She places each chair around the tables—one table in the Art area, one in the House Area, and one off to the side for Small Group Time. There is also a chair at the sign-in table, two chairs in the Writing Area, and two chairs at the computers.

Now that the chairs are ready, she does a quick spritz of the tables with a cleaner and paper towel (since the dirty chair legs were on the tables!) so the tables are nice and clean for children. Glancing around, she checks for other furniture that may need to be wiped off. She and her co-teacher, Mr. Charlie, clean the room every Friday afternoon, but sometimes furniture needs a quick swipe during the week.

Sarah takes one more long look over the classroom. This time she is looking for any safety issues that she needs to remedy. Standing at the front of the room, she can see in all of the corners and behind all of the shelves. All shelves in the room are low, so children cannot hide behind them and not be seen. There are no high shelves that could topple over, and none of the shelves are stacked high with materials or toys that could fall or cause the shelving to fall. All of the toys and materials are picked up, and as Sarah walks through the classroom, she looks at each of the shelves to make sure that all materials are put back in their proper places, so that children can find materials to work with easily.

She glances toward the parent board—a bulletin board she has created to share information with parents—and reminds herself that she needs to post the special schedule for Friday, which is Parent Day. She also jots a note in her planner to ask Mr. Charlie to locate a few adult-sized chairs they can bring into the room that day, for some of the elder grandparents who usually attend.

Satisfied now that the room is clean, tidy, orderly, and safe, she opens the sign-in book on the little table by the door and makes sure there are pencils in the pencil holder, and that each child's name card is in the file box. That done, she heads to her lesson plan book to double-check her plan for the day.

Teacher Sarah and her co-teacher Mr. Charlie know that the classroom environment is one of the most important elements of the teaching day. In fact, some people call the classroom environment "the third teacher" because if the environment is set up and arranged correctly for preschoolers, children learn just by playing and doing. Sarah wants to make sure her classroom is a safe and secure place for children to learn. She and Mr. Charlie have spent a lot of time considering how best to design and arrange their classroom space.

Design and physical arrangement

The design and physical arrangement of the preschool classroom is the starting point for delivering appropriate and engaging learning experiences for young children. When designed with careful thought and planning, the environment influences how children act and learn. When the classroom is organized and comfortable, children actively engage in the activities provided, and teachers interact with them productively throughout the day. In general, the classroom environment should:

- Be welcoming to children and parents
- Reflect children's families, culture, and community
- Allow children to see all work areas and move safely within the learning space
- Include enough materials for all children
- Allow children to locate, use, and return materials independently
- Encourage multiple types of play (constructive, creative, group play, etc.)

A well-designed classroom environment will support the development of autonomy and initiative by sending the following messages to children:

- This is a safe and comfortable place that I want to come to every day.
- I belong here and I am valued
- This is a place I can trust
- I can make friends and share
- I know what I'm expected to do
- I can do interesting work here
- I can find what I need and put things back where they belong
- I can make choices

Guidelines for Arranging Space

The following guidelines can help design a classroom arrangement that supports both teachers and children:

- In developing a floor plan, consider the fixed elements (doors, pillars or columns, stationary furniture that cannot be moved, restrooms, water sources, and so on) of the physical setting.

- Consider the traffic flow within and between the established work areas. Avoid large open spaces without purpose.

- Avoid placing furniture around the perimeter of the room to prevent leaving a "bowling alley" effect down the center.

- Provide space for each child to store personal belongings and items to take home at the end of the day. This may be a cubby or a bin and a hook for coats and jackets. Identify each cubby with child's name and perhaps a picture.

- Divide the space into well-defined work areas for distinctive types of play. Arrange active, noisy areas near each other and quieter areas in another part of the room.

- Choose names for the work areas that children and parents can understand. Label each area with pictures and words in both English and Native language.

- Establish visual boundaries between the work areas using low shelving, rugs, and other pieces of furniture. The areas should be clearly defined, and teachers should be able to visually monitor activities in areas, at all times. No hidden areas or cubbyholes.

- Plan the work areas to accommodate many types of play. The Art Area placed on tile near water makes cleanup more convenient, while carpet and floor cushions encourage comfortable time for exploring books in the Book Area.

- Include cozy, soft, quiet places where children can get away from the group and be by themselves.

- Consider placing tables in areas that could also be used for Small Group or snack times.

- Add materials and modify the learning areas throughout the year to address children's changing abilities and interests.

- Provide enough space for parents and children to work together in each learning area and to gather during PACT Time®.

- Plan for parents' comfort throughout the classroom by including adult-sized chairs, or children's chairs also designed for adult sitting.

Learning (Work) Areas

Dividing the classroom into work areas offers children choices of materials and activities, allows them to work with others in a small group setting, and supports them in focusing on their work in a manageable space. Teachers choose the kinds of work areas based in part on the space available in the room, the resources that are available, and the age and interests of students. Avoid having too many areas in a classroom, and consider that sometimes, one area may need to serve two purposes. For example, the Block Area may also be utilized as the Circle Time area in a small classroom. In many American Indian programs, space and classrooms can be limited, so be intentional about which areas are priority and how to incorporate them. Choose names for your areas that are simple, and relate to words that children use on a regular basis.

We provide the following suggestions, which work well in many American Indian preschool classrooms:

> House Area
> Block Area
> Art Area
> Book Area
> Writing Area
> Computer/Technology Area

For children not used to socializing in a group setting, these work areas and their simple names provide children with some familiarity—especially when they see the types of materials stored in each area. The House Area reminds them of home, with cooking activities, dolls, pillows, blankets, dress-up clothes, and the like. The Book Area has comfortable chairs, perhaps a bean bag chair, blankets and soft materials, and yes, books. The Block Area may remind children of things they see in their community—building materials, trucks, cars, stop signs, and more. The Art Area may be familiar to some, with paper, crayons, and other objects with which to create. We choose simple and familiar names for our work areas so that children can identify and more quickly become comfortable in the environment.

A Technology Area is often a welcome addition to the classroom. In this area children may explore computers, iPads and other digital devices, access audio books and listening stations, and more. The kinds of technology available may vary from school to school.

Variations on all Learning Areas are up to the teachers of the classroom and the needs of the students. We've seen classrooms combine areas, such as the Book/Writing Area, or the Technology/Writing Area. Some teachers combine writing with art. Three areas that are often added when classrooms have space are the Toy Area (small toys, manipulatives, puzzles, games), the Discovery Area (math and science materials), and the Music Area (listening to music, instruments, etc.). Other teachers weave these materials throughout the classroom.

When space allows, programs have created designated culture areas, which may include items specific to their own tribe and community, Native children's books, artifacts, traditional clothing, musical instruments, and more. Again, these learning areas would be specific to the community, and created with respect to the tribe and culture. Other classrooms choose to intersperse these items throughout the classroom—Native books in the Book Area, clothing and tools in the House or Block Area, and so on.

Children will need time to learn the routines for using the centers, managing the materials and moving about the classroom. At the beginning of the year, teachers might set up a few of the basic areas until children are comfortable navigating the classroom. In response to their increasing independence, changing interests and developing skills, additional work areas can be added during the year. Careful observation of how children engage in the various work areas can provide valuable information for making modifications to better address and challenge their developing abilities.

Some ideas for teachers—at the beginning of the year

As young children enter your classroom for the first time at the beginning of the school year, some will be excited to engage in new adventures and others will be unsure and reluctant to participate. The learning environment you establish must address the needs of every child, offering new and interesting experiences while ensuring familiarity, safety and security.

During the first couple of months of school, we want children to become familiar with the environment and learn to engage with materials and activities appropriately. To achieve these goals, we'll want to consider the following:

- *Create a welcoming environment* by including items that are familiar to children and reflect their families and homes.
  o A bulletin board that displays photographs of parents and children taken during home visits or orientation sessions.
  o A personal cubby for each child labeled with his photograph.
  o A blanket from home and favorite stuffed animal to be used for nap time – these will all communicate "you belong here" to your students.
- *Establish a few basic interest areas* by clearly defining and labeling the spaces within the classroom. To start, be sure to include the Block Area, House Area, Library Area, Art Area, and Technology Area. Starting the year with just five work areas will allow you to teach children about Work Time, making choices, and managing materials without overwhelming them. Other interest areas can be added once the basic routines are in place.

- ***Within each interest area, limit the quantity of materials at first*** until children understand their responsibility for accessing materials to work with and cleaning them up when they are finished. For example, perhaps the block area will have a set of wooden blocks, farm animals, vehicles and people figures at the beginning of the year. Additional types of blocks and other props can be added gradually after children understand how to return the blocks to the storage shelves and sort the props into bins.
- ***Be sure materials in each interest area are stored in an organized and clearly labeled way.*** When all shelves and containers are clearly labeled, children will quickly learn to independently manage classroom materials.
- From the beginning of the year, ***place relevant books in each interest area*** and model their use as you interact with children during Work Time. The integrated use of literacy materials is a foundational element of a preschool classroom. As you read stories to the dolls in the House Area or refer to a book about buildings in the Block Area children are learning about the importance of literacy in their lives.

Choosing Materials

Classroom work areas are engaging for children when teachers carefully select and organize the materials in each area. Choose materials that are developmentally and culturally appropriate, and of interest to children. Open-ended items—those materials that can be used in a variety of ways, with no one particular way to use—encourage children to explore and experiment. Real and found items—items located in the home or community, such as leaves, paper towel rolls, empty food containers, old purses—can encourage a sense of imagination and creativity in play. Reflecting the experiences and culture of the children honors the heritage and community they know best. Inviting parents to choose some of the materials, and loan or donate items to the classroom, gives them a sense of ownership and belonging in their child's room.

Guidelines for Choosing Materials:
- Choose materials that reflect the children's interests. Maintain a supply of additional materials that can be introduced throughout the year as interests change.
- Choose materials that are appropriate for the range of children's developmental levels represented in the class. Rotate items through the work areas during the year to keep up with children's developing abilities.
- Provide items that can be used in a variety of ways. Containers of "found" or real materials (stones, shells, nuts/bolts, buttons, feathers, etc.) are open-ended and can be located throughout the work areas.
- Bring elements of the natural world, such as plants, animals, and objects from nature, into the classroom to encourage exploration and engage the senses.

- Choose interesting materials that support the different types of play that are typical of young children. Children should be able to manipulate and transform objects, take things apart and put them together, create, build, experiment and use objects to represent other things.

- Maintain an adequate supply of materials so all children working in an area can participate without conflicts over limited resources. This may include having duplicates of more popular items.

- Ensure that books and writing tools are available in all work areas. Reference books, books for reading, paper, notebooks, pencils, and markers encourage children to expand their use of literacy skills and document their learning in a variety of ways.

- Choose materials that reflect the experiences and cultures of the children in the program. Incorporate items from the culture or the community as appropriate. For example: saddles, boots, fishing gear, canoes, woven baskets or rugs, jewelry or clothing for dress-up, and Native posters, sayings and photographs. Connect with the school's cultural teacher and other outside cultural resources to enhance the learning environment.

- Provide opportunities for parents to choose, make or donate materials for the classroom. Include family photos and items from home in the classroom work areas so children feel that it is truly their classroom.

- Use bulletin boards and other display spaces to showcase children's work. Involve children in choosing the work they'd like to share, include their names and words about the item, and change the display regularly. Photos of children working in the various areas of the classroom can be a way to share information about your curriculum and daily routine with visitors.

- Make sure the materials are safe, clean, and well maintained. Replace worn or broken items as necessary.

Guidelines for Storing Materials:
- Avoid clutter and the temptation to provide too many materials in the work areas. It's more important to offer attractive and interesting materials to challenge children at different levels of development. Keep a supply of materials in storage and rotate them into the centers as the year progresses.

- Store materials so they are accessible to children. Use low shelving with baskets or bins to gather objects that are alike.
- Use see-through or open containers to store materials in plain view.
- Make sure materials are organized and consistently stored in the same place.
- Label shelves and containers with pictures, symbols, words (in English and Native language), and real objects, so children can easily find and put away materials independently.
- When adding materials to the classroom, consider introducing the materials in Small Group Time. After children have had an opportunity to explore the new materials, involve them in deciding where to store the new materials.

Helping Children Clean-up and Put Away Materials

Teacher Sarah knows that learning can sometimes be messy, which is why she and Mr. Charlie have a system worked out for cleaning up after Work Time. The children know this system, too.

After almost an hour of Work Time, Miss Sarah sets a timer and says to the children, "We have five minutes to finish our work before cleanup. Joe, will you remind me when this timer goes off? That means it's cleanup time."

"Yes, Miss Sarah!" Joe glances to the kitchen timer while he and Jamie work on getting the animals in the zoo. Finally, the timer goes off and Joe says, "Miss Sarah! It's cleanup time!"

She smiles and reaches for the timer. "Mr. Charlie, should we put on the cleanup song?" He puts a CD in the player—it's the same cleanup song they play every day. When children hear that song, they know what to do next. (Some, of course, a little slower than others.)

Clean-up time takes about another five minutes. Sometimes when the children are slower at cleanup, Miss Sarah sets the timer again, or challenges them to a game of getting cleaned up, "before the cleanup song ends." This gives children an end-point for cleanup, so they can keep on schedule and move on to the next block in their daily routine.

"Remember, as soon as your area is cleaned up, let's come together at the circle," Mr. Charlie says. He is leading the review part of Work Time today.

Some tips for making cleanup time more productive:

- Think of the children's classroom as being organized like a big puzzle. If all shelves and containers are clearly labeled so that children can see where an item lives, clean-up time can happen quickly and orderly. Help children know how to work the puzzle—to look for pictures, labels, and real objects to guide them. Pretend you are playing a big matching game!
- Early in the year, practice with children putting items away in the smaller areas.
- Provide some guidelines about cleaning up. When children finish in one area, they put toys away before moving to the next area. This means that teachers and co-teachers are observant and nearby to guide children when they stray.
- Use a timer or a device that signals a warning time, and a clean-up time.
- Whatever devices teachers use for clean-up, they should use them consistently to form the daily habit to cleanup on time, and without struggle.

Basic Equipment and Classroom Materials

- 3 Round 48-60" tables to seat 5-6 children each (two for learning areas and small groups, one for house area)
- 15-20 children's classroom chairs (sized for 4-year olds, and able to fit adults who may visit the classroom)
- 2 small tables for assorted materials, listening area, miscellaneous purposes
- 2 rectangular tables for computers or printer, or preschool designed/appropriate computer table(s)
- 5-6 wooden 30" high shelving units (preferably on wheels for ease of movement)
- 2 wooden 30" high storage shelves with see-through bins for art supplies and toys (preferably on wheels)

- Easy access to copy machine (not in the classroom)
- Telephone for calls to families, community resources, etc. (not necessarily in classroom)
- Filing cabinet with lock (for storing sensitive and confidential family information)
- Storage cabinets for teacher storage
- 2-3 children's book display racks (front facing display with the covers visible)

- Big book display rack
- Cubbies for children's belongings (for 15-20 children)
- 15-20 mats for rest time
- Tricycles, wagons, balls, parachute
- 2-3 large rugs (to define learning areas—recommend rugs with patterns that are not too busy or distracting)
- Child-themed posters and positive messages (Native posters)
- Miscellaneous materials for teachers (stacking trays and storage trays, paper, scissors, tape dispenser, pens, pencils, glue, etc.)
- Large classroom clock

Learning Area Furniture and Materials

House Area: This area should promote dramatic play. There should be a variety of materials available to promote children's role-play, pretending and learning.

- Wooden model refrigerator, stove, sink, cupboard, a couch, comfortable chair, rocking chair, ironing board
- Wooden 30" high shelves
- Native dolls; baby clothes, bib, bottles, blankets, sturdy doll highchair, cradle
- Dress-up clothes—include items that reflect the local culture; items that represent various jobs in the community; hanging storage for the clothes (pegboard, hooks)
- Shopping cart
- Full-length children's safety mirror
- 48" round table and chairs (Do not buy small house area table—remember adults and children will need to fit at the table during PACT Time.)
- Real materials—donated or locally purchased items are more useful than play items: 2 telephones, appliances with cords removed (toaster, mixer, unbreakable coffee pot, blow dryer, clock radio, etc.), plastic bowls, plates, real utensils, pots, pans, skillet, etc.
- Child-sized broom, mop, dustpan
- Special kitchen items that reflect the homes and culture of the children (parents may suggest and/or donate these items

Art Area:
- 2 easels with attached paint trays
- Paint smocks (can be purchased or homemade)

- Sealable paint pots
- Washable tempera paints
- Glue, staplers, tape (masking, scotch, colored)
- Small scissors, hole punchers, eye droppers, tweezers
- Paint brushes
- 48-60" table and chairs
- Sand and water table (9" deep) and materials (funnel, sifter, baster, etc.)
- Assorted paper (construction, wax, finger paint, tissues, assorted colors)
- Play dough, cookie cutters, rolling pins
- Assorted art junk (feathers, pom-poms, letter shapes, stencils, number shapes, things to glue on pictures, ribbon, stickers, rubber stamps and stamp pads, etc.)

Writing/Computer (Technology) Area:
- Pens, pencils, markers, crayons and other writing tools
- Variety of paper for writing, drawing
- Writing slates, stencils, stamps
- White boards and markers
- Envelopes
- Chalkboards and chalk
- Journals, notebooks, home-made blank books
- Book making materials – paper, staplers, hole punches, tape, key rings, yarn
- Calendar
- Real life writing materials – checks, lists, note cards, sticky notes, junk mail, invitations, etc.
- Computers with Internet access
- Laptops, iPads, or other digital devices
- Preschool appropriate software, or access to downloadable or Internet-based web sites—children's games, alphabet, stories, interactive reading, phonological awareness, math, etc.)
- Printer, or access to a printer (not necessarily in room)
- Digital camera (for collecting work samples development, sharing with parents, etc.)

Book Area:

- 5 books per child minimum - Assorted books (story, rhyme, wordless, predictable, non-fiction, photograph, Native stories, alphabet, counting, concept, fairy tales, etc.)
- Books that reflect the local culture, language and ethnic groups, family structures, regional settings, homes and languages of the families
- 25 big books (assorted, repetitive, word play, interactive)
- Books written by children, parents and staff
- 2 wooden forward-facing book display racks
- Beanbag chairs, floor pillows, couch or soft chair
- Large rug to define area
- Small wooden table for listening area
- CD player with books and recorded stories, including stories recorded by children, parents, and staff
- Puppets and puppet stand
- Flannel board and felt story figures

Block Area:

- Wooden 30" high shelves for organizing materials
- Assorted blocks (wooden, brick, Duplo, foam)
- Vehicles (buses, trucks, cars, tractors, boats, planes, etc.)
- Animals (zoo, farm, pets, dinosaurs)
- People for play (bendable, Native, real-looking)
- Fences, bridges, barns, road signs, etc.
- Books about construction, buildings, bridges, cars, boats, architecture
- Maps and blueprints
- Clipboards, paper, pencils
- Large carpet to define area

Miscellaneous items that could be incorporated into existing centers, or create separate centers, such as Toy, Puzzle, Math, Discovery/Science, Music, etc.

- Puzzles
- Lacing materials
- Counting materials (dinosaurs, bears, assorted manipulatives)
- Stringing beads
- Pegs and pegboards
- Alphabet manipulatives, games, and puzzles
- 1 inch cubes
- 30" high wooden shelves for organizing materials
- See-through bins to store materials
- Balance scales
- Geoboards
- Large magnets
- Magnifying glasses
- Musical instruments
- Objects for exploration (binoculars, magnifying glasses, thermometers)

Outdoor Environment:

Every school's outdoor environment will differ based on available space, terrain, climate, and resources. What follows here are suggestions for creating an outdoor environment that supports children's learning and development in a variety of areas and that is viewed as an extension of the preschool classroom.

General outdoor play spaces:

- Climbing area
- Sand area
- Water area
- Building area
- A covered area to protect from rain or sun (in desert areas)
- Paved or hard surfaces for riding

Outdoor play equipment

- Jungle gym or other climbing apparatus
- Slides
- Hanging bars
- Tunnels
- Obstacle course
- Ramps
- Over/under platform and bridges
- Tricycles, scooters or other wheeled toys
- Wagons
- Storage shed
- Soft material like sand or bark under equipment

Props for sand play

- Sand box
- Plastic and metal buckets
- Pails with handles
- Shovels, spoons and scoops of all sizes
- Old trucks, cars, etc.
- Funnels and sifters
- Pots, pans and molds
- Wheelbarrows
- Old or plastic blocks
- Natural objects such as stones, shells and leaves

Props for water play

- Spray bottles
- Food coloring
- Siphons or pumps
- Boats, people, animals
- Squeeze bottles and pitchers
- Egg beaters
- Whisks
- Plastic straws
- Plastic tubing
- Eyedroppers
- Corks
- Sponges
- Bubble-blowing materials (paper, straws, solution, etc.).

Garden area

- Several sets of hand-held garden tools
- Hoes and rakes
- Gardening gloves
- A wheelbarrow
- Seeds and plants
- Watering can
- Books on gardening and plants

The CIRCLES® Classroom Environment Checklist

This checklist represents the kinds of preschool environment best practices often seen in high quality preschool learning environments. The checklist encompasses all children, inclusive of the needs of children with disabilities and diverse learning styles, and those who are dual language learners (DLL). Indicate your level of practices in these areas below.

A classroom environment supports preschool children's growth, development, and learning. Is each item below routine practice for you, or an area of improvement?	Routine Practice	Area of Improvement
Ensure a warm environment that reflects children's homes and lives, where they can listen to and interact with peers, staff and parents throughout the day.		
The room is equipped with low shelves and furniture, dividing the room into specific work areas. The work areas include a minimal of 5 areas: • House Area • Book Area • Art Area • Block Area • Writing/Computer Area		
If space allows, other work areas are added according to the needs of the children and goals of the program, for example: Discovery (Science, Math), Toy, Puzzle, Music areas.		
The environment is safe and free from safety hazards, such as tall shelves that could topple, materials and equipment stored on high shelves, blocked exits, or hidden areas in the classroom.		
The environment is family focused, provides space for parents, and has an open-door policy for parents.		
The environment reflects the Native culture of the community of the school, and of the families who attend school.		
Materials are organized and located on shelves or in clear boxes. Materials are labeled in Native language and in English.		
Provide listening areas with songs, stories, and other listening games in a variety of media (software, books on tape/CD, Smart Board, etc.).		

Provide props, materials, and experiences that build on children's interests and encourage talking, listening, and storytelling/retelling in dramatic play, block and other classroom areas.		
Provide books and literacy connections in all areas of the classroom.		
Add new books and materials on curriculum topics to all classroom areas periodically.		
Provide writing materials/tools, and alphabet and letter/word tools throughout all areas of the classroom.		
Equip a writing area with a variety of writing tools and paper for experimentation.		
Display functional print throughout the classroom, such as: names on cubbies, attendance sign-in charts, pet names, menus, message boards, signs and labels, maps, etc.		
Display purposeful environmental print (signs and labels) in both children's home languages (first) and English, throughout the classroom.		
Adults use responsive adult-child interactive strategies to model good oral language practices with children throughout the day.		
Prominently display children's work at their eye level.		
Provide inviting spaces throughout the classroom for children to read with their friends, parents, and other adults, or on their own.		
Equip dramatic play areas with props and materials that encourage talking, listening, and pretending.		
Provide an inviting, orderly and accessible Book Area: Stocked with about five books per child • Books displayed on open shelves, covers out, at children's eye level • Books easily accessible for children • Comfortable/soft areas for reading • Books in children's home languages and other multi-cultural books		

The Morning Routine

> Before she left school the night before, Teacher Sarah pulled out the materials and books she would need for Circle Time the next morning, and for her Small Groups later in the day. She placed the books next to her spot in the Circle Time circle, turned on her Smart Board, and cued the software for taking attendance. Checking the planning book, she then sorted the Small Group materials into baggies for the children, prepared a tray with items she would need to teach with, and organized all of her materials on a shelf next to her Small Group table.
>
> While she was doing that, Mr. Charlie, her co-teacher, arrived and started his preparations for the day too. He consulted the planning book, gathered the materials for his Small Group in a similar way, and organized them. Once finished, Mr. Charlie headed off toward the cafeteria to be with the children and parents who had arrived early for breakfast.
>
> One last task—Teacher Sarah read through the two books she planned to use this morning one more time. She took a moment to jot down some comments and questions she would like to use for sparking dialogue on sticky notes and posted them on the book pages. Then, she wrote her morning message on the white board in the Circle Time area, and looked up to see the first of her children arriving.
>
> Time to start their daily routine.

Daily routines form the basic structure of a preschooler's day. Consistent daily routines help children make sense of their world and maintain order in their lives. Children should be able to predict what will happen next and begin to understand their role in the activities of the day. When routines are predictable, children feel safe and in control of their environment. This comfort level allows them to explore the classroom and take on new challenges a bit at a time, and it puts them in a better place to manage change when it occurs.

Whether American Indian, or non-American Indian, many children arrive at preschool with no sense of routine—at home or at school. Some children entering preschool programs have difficulty navigating the day at first, so plan to introduce routines slowly and be patient. At the beginning of the year, make your routine as simple as possible. As the children grow into the consistent habits of their day, you can add more detail. Start simple, but establish routines right from the start.

The preschool daily routine should provide a balance of activities that meet the developmental and individual needs of the children in the classroom. Time should be provided daily for children to work independently and with other children, in small groups, in large groups, and with teachers. There should be a balance of active and quiet times throughout the day. Active learning, choice and decision making by children are built into each part of the day.

In general, routines are designed to provide children:

- Security and predictability in an environment they can trust to meet their needs
- A variety of experiences that address all areas of development
- Opportunities to work in large and small groupings with other children
- Opportunities to work by themselves and develop independence
- Opportunities to make choices and decisions
- Opportunities to plan and reflect on their experiences
- Opportunities to exercise both large muscles and small muscles
- A sense of time and sequence as they move through the day's activities
- A social atmosphere for play, talk, laughter and problem solving with others

Over the following pages, we will demonstrate and describe each of the following segments of the preschool day:

- Arrival and Departure
- Circle Time
- Small Group Time
- Wonder-Work-Share Time
- Meal and Snack Times
- Outside Time
- PACT Time®
- Rest/Quiet Time

The CIRCLES Morning Routine looks like this:
- **Circle Time (5-15 minutes)**
- **Small Group Time (10-20 minutes)**
- **Work Time (Wonder-Work-Share) (50-60 minutes)**

In a CIRCLES Classroom we want to focus intentionally on the children's Morning Routine. We recommend that The Morning Routine be planned and implemented in a specific way. Children are ready to learn in the mornings after they have had breakfast and have greeted their friends. Children are fresh and eager to get started early in the day. The CIRCLES Morning Routine maximizes children's varied approaches to learning and learning styles. The CIRCLES Morning Routine allows for individual, small group, and large group interactions. Time for observation, experimentation, and reflection are also included within this time frame.

The CIRCLES Morning Routine lasts approximately one hour and thirty/forty minutes. This varies from classroom to classroom depending on children's abilities and the time of the year. The CIRCLES Morning Routine works best when the segments of the morning are done in sequence and within recommended time allotments. In a true CIRCLES classroom model, this block of time would not be interrupted by other activities or snack time. Plan other activities and meal times around this block of time. It is important to protect your Morning Routine and to be consistent with how it is implemented daily

The following chart describes the process with more detail.

The CIRCLES Morning Routine

The chart below outlines the recommended sequence of events of the morning routine for children, after arrival and before lunch, utilizing the CIRCLES teaching strategy. By planning the morning experiences in this order, teachers are honoring the varied learning styles of the American Indian children in the classroom. The morning time is also when children are generally the most alert, and they will function and perform better during this part of the day.

Part of the Day	What teachers do	What children do
Circle Time	Briefly share the **Big Idea**. Show or talk about the focus/theme of the day.	**Observe and Listen** Sometimes ask questions.
Small Group Time (SGT)	**Model/Demonstrate** the Big Idea. Teachers use self-talk to talk about what they are doing.	**Observe and Listen** Sometimes ask questions.
	Talk about what children are doing (parallel talk) and encourage discussion. Remember, some children may be processing or reflecting during this time, and may not ask or respond to questions. Teachers observe while children "do." Make sure the SGT is an Active Learning experience.	**Children "Do"** under teacher supervision, observation, and perhaps some guidance.
Work Time (WT)	**Transition to Work Time** (planning for WT). Help children plan for Work Time. Children may continue working with the SGT materials or choose to work elsewhere. Talk with children about where the materials will be located during Work Time. Allow children to experiment with the materials on their own, without teacher supervision, during WT. Trial and error and mistakes are okay and encouraged—this is learning. Don't worry if children do not use the materials today—they may come back to them another day. Keep materials from all SGTs for the week available all week in a prominent place. Later, blend them into the classroom environment. Continue to observe children and monitor to assess informally. Jot down anecdotal notes daily.	Continue time for children to **Experiment Individually** with materials without adult supervision in the learning areas. They may also choose to work with the materials collaboratively, with other children. This is okay.
Reflection	Provide time and space for children to **reflect** on their own, or with small or large groups of children. Use a variety of reflection strategies.	Children gather in the circle with teachers and reflect on their experiences with the materials. Children choose when to share. Children reflect in various ways, and not all ways are verbal.

Segments Of The Daily Routine

Arrival and Departure

When four-year-old Joe enters his classroom, he bursts through the door with Mom close. He's a second-year preschooler and is very familiar with the classroom, the teachers, and the daily routine. He and his mom are just coming back from breakfast in the cafeteria. He glances back at Mom and says, "Come on! Let's get a book to read."

Mom knows Joe loves choosing a book first thing in the morning after breakfast, but she redirects. "Joe, we need to do a couple of things first. Remember?"

Joe grins and tips his head to the side. "Yeah." He heads to his cubby—the one with his name printed on it above his picture—and hangs up his coat. Reaching into the top, he pulls out an art project he made the day before and hands it to her. "It's dry. Can you take it home?"

Joe's mom takes the paper. "Sure. Now what's next?"

Joe heads to the sign-in desk. On the way, he waves. "Hi Miss Sarah!" His teacher smiles and waves back, then turns to another child. He settles into the desk, leaning into it on his elbows. He picks up a pencil in the cup by the sign-in notebook, and then reaches for the index card box. He finds his name card and looks up at his mom. "Tomorrow I'll write my name without the card."

She smiles and says, "You can do it." She watches Joe sign in, noticing how much better he is getting at writing his name. He's just turned four but is growing so fast.

"Now the book." Joe takes his mom by the hand and leads her to the book basket in the center of the carpet. They sit on the floor and his mom says, "Just one today, Joe. I'm a little late for work."

He nods and they pick out a book about zoo animals. Joe's mom reads the story while other children arrive. Gradually, several children—some with parents and some not—sit in the circle reading together. Joe's mom loves this time with him. Since she works, she can't come back for PACT Time later in the day, but she makes it a point to bring Joe to school as early as possible so they can read together. They finish the story and she leans in to whisper, "I have to go now. But you know I'll be back on time."

He pulls back and looks at her. "Yep. Right after rest time. Will you read to me again then?" She nods and kisses his cheek, then leaves. Joe settles in, his attention now on his teacher.

Although they are not always viewed as parts of the instructional day, *arrival and departure times* are important. The routines you develop can have an impact on the tone set for the day and how children and parents remember the day's experiences.

As parents arrive with their children, be sure they know where to find children's cubbies for storing their personal items. Most classrooms require that parents sign in to a log or notebook located near the door. An excellent literacy activity that also formalizes the arrival process is to have the children "sign in," as well. Have large paper on a table near the door, with name cards for each child and a variety of writing implements. The process of signing in is more important here than the quality of the child's written name, but with name cards available as models, teachers often see great improvement in name writing as the year progresses.

Help parents recognize the importance of a goodbye hug and a cheerful departure with a promise to be back later in the day. Have a plan, especially at the beginning of the year, to help parents with those tearful or difficult good-byes—providing strategies to help the child feel safe in the classroom and to reduce worry and anxiety for the parents.

> **The routines you develop with children set the tone for the day, and how children and parents remember the day's experiences.**

Recognize that children will arrive gradually in the morning and have a transition activity planned for that initial period. Often, teachers will have a few limited options for children to choose from—like puzzles set out on a table and books available on the carpet for browsing. It's always a good idea to have one teacher greeting parents and children at the door as they arrive and the other teacher engaging with children in the selected transition activities.

Departure routines are equally important for helping parents and children bring the school day to a pleasant close. Provide children with adequate notice when the day is ending so they can bring their play or projects to a satisfactory close. Be sure anything that is going home is placed in the children's cubby or backpack and that parents know where to check for work and notes each day. Having one teacher engage the children in an activity is important to keep them from anxiously wondering when their parent is going to come for them. The other teacher can greet parents at the door, provide a positive comment about their children's experiences that day, and send families on their way.

Separation anxiety. Arrival and drop-off times for very young children just learning about preschool and group social situations can be very scary—for both parents and children! Children who are unsure about separating from their parents exhibit their uneasiness by clinging, crying/screaming, and sometimes with physical reactions such as hitting and running. We have to remember that the anxiety induced by separating from parents is a real thing, and that we are probably all going to deal with it at some time, or another.

The best course of defense is to guide the parent through the process. Parents may also be anxious about leaving their children for a while, so they may need as much reassurance as the children that all will be fine.

Here are some proactive steps to help everyone deal with separation anxiety:

- Talk to parents ahead of time and discuss any of their concerns about leaving their children at preschool.
- Assure parents that all will be fine, but listen to their legitimate concerns.
- Make a plan of action with the parent, agreeing to the following (or similar):
    - The parent agrees to a routine at drop-off and to stick to the routine. The routine could be something like this: Enter classroom, child puts belongings in cubby and signs in, Mom kisses child goodbye and says, "I'll see you this afternoon," and leaves.
    - The parent agrees that no amount of crying that happens (on child or parent part!) will change the routine. They will move forward and leave the classroom, as planned.
    - The teacher/co-teacher will divert child's attention and support the child through the transition until calm.
    - The teacher and parent agree on a time limit to allow the child to calm down. If the child does not significantly calm down, say within 15 minutes, the teacher will call the parent to let him/her know.

Remember, the more quickly the child gets into the routine of arrival and parent departure, the better. When the parent refuses to leave or keeps coming back in "to check" the cycle has to start all over again. Eliminating as many times as possible for parent-child separation during the day is always a good idea.

Circle Time

> "Boys and girls," Miss Sarah says, "All of our friends are here now—let's get started. I have a really fun book to share today. Everyone comfortable? Remember, let's put our listening ears on in case we need to talk about the story."
>
> Teacher Sarah knows that preschool children need an activity to bring them together as a group after the hectic few minutes of arrival. It helps them create a community of learning together. Since parents and busses arrive over a 20-minute period, she likes providing choices while they wait. All children sign in each morning. Some like to read books, and some work puzzles at the puzzle table. Now that everyone is here, it is time to get started.
>
> She reads a book today at the beginning of Circle Time, but doesn't ask a lot of questions since it is a new book to the children. The book is called Eating the Alphabet and she is introducing it today by showing the pictures and talking about the letters and illustrations. The goal for today's Circle Time is simply to introduce the book and get the children familiar with it. She has plans to come back to this book again in Small Group, and later today in the PACT Time closing circle.
>
> She tries to read new books three or four times during the week so that children have time to explore and think about the concepts and ideas shared in the story. Teacher Sarah continues Circle Time with a few more group activities. First, they take attendance using the SMART Board, and then sing a rhyming alphabet song. They share a daily message on the white board, and then Miss Sarah leads a discussion about the weather. Finally, they close with a Native book the class read together last week. This time, Miss Sarah asks questions using dialogic reading prompts, and focuses on some vocabulary words she wants children to remember. She is ready with discussion questions to spark dialogue, but knows that some children may not be ready to discuss yet.
>
> At the end of Circle Time, Teacher Sarah says, "Let's look at our schedule for today." She points to the left-to-right picture blocks posted underneath the chalkboard behind her. "Let's see, we just finished Circle Time. What's next?"

Circle Time, a teacher-led whole group experience, is held at the beginning of the day as a way to bring the class together as a learning community and to set the tone and purpose for the day. Limited to 5-20 minutes (depending on when in the year it occurs) Circle Time can include a variety of elements designed to meet the needs of each class:

- ***Welcome song:*** A familiar song that recognizes the children by name is a favorite way to start Circle Time each day. It signals the beginning of the school day and becomes a comfortable routine in which everyone can participate.

- ***Share The Big Idea.*** This is a great time to provide a short experience for children that draws their attention to The Big Idea, or the focus of the week. This is when you plant the seeds for more activities to come throughout the day. Provide the big picture, a global and visual view, of your targeted focus for the day or week. This Big Idea is likely attached to the preschool standards and to the goals/needs of the children in the classroom.

- ***Attendance:*** The process of taking attendance is an opportunity to involve children in recognizing their names in writing, as well as counting and classifying. Teachers use a variety of strategies that may evolve during the year as children's needs and abilities change.

- ***Schedule for the day:*** When the daily routine has been posted where the children can see it, it can be reviewed as a reminder of what will be happening that day. This is particularly important on days when there is a special activity or other change in the normal routine. Concepts of time, such as morning/afternoon, before/after, or early/late can be emphasized in this process.

- ***Literacy Experiences:*** Circle Time is a good opportunity to share stories, teach finger plays, and sing songs. Dialogic Reading experiences are appropriate here, as are group discussions and the sharing of ideas. Big Books work best in the large group setting so all children can see the text and illustrations. Writing modeled by the teacher on large chart paper can record stories, lists, ideas, or questions from the children. Key to these experiences is an emphasis on speaking, listening, reading, and writing.

- ***Music and Movement:*** To ensure a variety of activities that address a range of developmental areas, introduce movement and dance into your Circle Time routine. Children will quickly develop favorites as they move to the music and build their motor skills.

- ***Other group activities:*** Depending on the size of the group and the developmental levels of the children, teachers often add the review of other concepts to their Circle Time routines. Using visual cues posted on the walls, children may review vocabulary of color, number or size in English and Native languages. They may name letters or numbers or practice counting skills. These kinds of activities should be chosen carefully with attention to the developmental needs of the children and used only when they are appropriate for all students.

> Circle Time, held at the beginning of the day, is a way to bring the class together as a learning community.

Many teachers choose to hold another brief Circle Time at the end of the school day. One more story or song can be shared in the large group. This is also a wonderful opportunity for children to recall events of the day and reflect on all they accomplished. The teacher might record in writing some of the children's thoughts and encourage them to share their reflections with their families.

Why Post the Daily Routine for Children?

In the previous scenario, at the end of Circle Time, Teacher Sarah said, "Let's look at our schedule for today." She pointed to the left-to-right picture blocks posted underneath the chalkboard behind her

and added, "Let's see, we just finished Circle Time. What's next?"

> Joe, ever the eager beaver, raises his hand, but this time Miss Sarah asks another child. "Serena, you are so quiet, but I bet you know what's next. Can you show me?" Serena smiles and nods, and turns around to face the daily routine blocks. She moves the marker and quietly says, "Small Group."
>
> Miss Sarah smiles, realizing this is the first time Serena has spoken in front of the class. "That's right, Serena. Good job!" She gives her a hug before she sits back with the group.
>
> Tate interrupts. "But I'm hungry. Isn't it lunch time yet?"
>
> Miss Sarah gives him a puzzled look. "Hm." Tate was the last to arrive, and she wonders if he missed breakfast. She glances at Mr. Charlie who nods back. "Maybe we should look at that schedule again. Want to look at it with me, Tate?" They look at the routine blocks and she adds, "Where is lunch on the schedule, Tate?" He points to the block. "And where are we now?" He points to the Small Group block. "Yes. So how many blocks between Small Group and lunch?"
>
> Tate frowns and says, "It's the next one. After Work Time."
>
> Miss Sarah smiles and adds, "Just one more block. That's right. Tate, would you go check with Mr. Charlie about something?" He nods and he and Mr. Charlie step away from the group for a moment. While Miss Sarah talks with the children, she watches Mr. Charlie get a breakfast bar from the cabinet and settle Tate into a seat at the table in the House Area.

Posting the daily routine

A visual representation of the daily routine should be posted at the children's eye level in your classroom and referred to often as you move throughout the day. There are many ways routines can be depicted—often simple drawings or photographs of each segment of the day are paired with a word label that matches it. Keep the schedule simple and only represent the larger blocks of time, for example:

- Circle Time
- Small Group
- Work Time
- Lunch
- Outside
- PACT Time
- Rest
- Closing Circle

Post the daily routine from left to right on the wall at the children's eye level. Refer to it often throughout the day.

Times are not important for children right now, so we suggest leaving those off. The visual representation, and the order in which the blocks are posted, are the important pieces of information. Remember, the blocks of times should be posted from left-to-right, the same way we learn to read. Avoid schedules in lists or circles, and those that provide information that children do not need to know. You can post a more detailed schedule for parents, where they can see it.

The sequence of daily activities can be reviewed at the beginning of the day and children's attention can be drawn to "what comes next" as the day progresses. Although the routine is consistent from day to day, it also must be flexible enough to accommodate special events or other necessary changes. When children know what to expect on a typical day, they can more easily manage changes to the routine as they occur. In some classes, teachers manipulate the daily routine cards to show children how a special day might be slightly different than the norm.

Small Group Time

"So, I guess we better get to Small Group, right?" Quickly, Miss Sarah provides instructions to the children. Some of them go with Mr. Charlie to his table and some with her. Teacher Sarah knows that in a few minutes, three children will be leaving to go with Miss Tonya for speech therapy, so she has taken that into consideration when planning for her groups. In her group, she has children who are headed to kindergarten next year, and Mr. Charlie has a group of younger children, most of whom need extra work on fine motor skills.

When both groups are settled, she calls to Tate, who is finishing eating his snack, and says, "You can join me here as soon as you are finished, Tate." He nods and crumples up his paper, washes his hands, and joins Miss Sarah at the table.

In both small groups, Teacher Sarah and Mr. Charlie have planned to use specific materials and have a goal in mind for what they would like to see children do with the materials—but they also know the children may have other ideas too. That is okay.

Both teachers begin their Small Groups by reading a few more pages of Eating the Alphabet. The focus for Miss Sarah's group is to practice identifying and matching upper and lower case letters. Later in the week she will add writing the upper and lower case letters. Mr. Charlie's group will focus on letters too, but his goal is more about manipulating them, than identifying and matching. He has added play dough to his list of materials for the children to use. He wants to help them work on building their fine motor skills, while playing with the letters.

After Miss Sarah has read a little more of the story, she puts her book down flat on the table. Then she gets some magnetic letters out of her baggie, and with the children, starts matching the letters to the ones on the pages in the book. She lays an upper case A on top of the upper case A in the book. She provides several more examples, using self-talk to talk about what she is doing while she is doing it, and while the children watch and listen. "I'm putting this red upper case A on this red upper case A on this page."

Although she doesn't want to guide everything children do with the materials, and she doesn't want them to follow her idea step-for-step, she knows that many American Indian children have learning styles that are best supported by seeing the big idea first, so she provides them with a clear picture of what she wants them to do.

Next, she hands each child a baggie of upper and lower case magnetic letters and their own Eating the Alphabet book. She says, "I wonder if you can match the letters too?" The children are allowed to explore their book and materials, finding letters in the book to match the letters in their baggies. Miss Sarah keeps active learning principles in mind so that she can support them. She wants the children to manipulate the materials, explore, and experiment in ways that make sense to them. She watches and observes how they use them. Often, she will jot down anecdotal notes during this time, to help her gauge which children are catching on, and which ones need more practice.

Miss Sarah puts her materials away while the children work. She wanted to provide them with the big idea, but she doesn't want them to copy what she did. She allows them to work and ask questions if they want. She provides support when, and if, needed, but doesn't overpower the conversation at the table with her words. She is more interested in hearing dialogue and conversation from the children and knows that if all of the airspace is filled with her words, children may feel there is no space left for their words.

Sometimes during Small Group, she'll have some additional materials close by to add to the table, if she thinks it would be beneficial. Children often want something else and ask for it. "Miss Sarah, I need scissors to finish this. And tape. Can I get some from the Art Area?" Teacher Sarah always says, "Yes."

After about 15 minutes of Small Group practice and experimentation, Miss Sarah signals that it is time to finish their work. She says, "Let's tidy up our spaces in front of us and put our letters back in the baggies." She wants children to always get in the habit of cleaning up after an activity. Next, she adds, "We'll keep these materials here on the table, and some of you may choose to continue working with them during Work Time. Okay?"

By giving permission to extend the time children can experiment with and manipulate the materials into Work Time, Miss Sarah is respecting the children's need for reflective learning.

Small Group Time is the part of the day when teachers can be intentional in their instruction with children. Teachers work with children in small groups to extend learning, challenge children's thinking, introduce new concepts, develop problem-solving skills, and help children learn to work together. This is an excellent time to focus on those school readiness skills defined by preschool standards.

Small Group Time is defined as a segment of the daily routine in which a group of 5-10 children meet with a teacher or co-teacher, at a consistent time and place, to work with materials selected by the teacher. It offers a balance to other parts of our day where children work individually or in whole group activities. Small group time occurs every day for 15-20 minutes and typically involves splitting the class between the teacher and co-teacher to create two groups.

Small Group Time is a part of the day when teachers can be intentional in their instruction with children.

Small Group Time works best when the groups are consistent from day-to-day and children work with the same teacher for a period of weeks. This allows children to develop relationships with the other members of the group as well as with the teacher. Often, groups are created based on developmental levels, with the older children working in one group and the younger children in another. Of course age is not always an indicator of developmental level, so teachers plan groups accordingly, and sometimes it may be beneficial for a child to change groups. Planning small group activities is more manageable when the range of developmental levels within the group is somewhat limited.

Teachers plan Small Group Time by considering the needs and interests of the children. Small Group Time often focuses on supporting a specific skill from the preschool standards, learning how to use new materials, or exploring new ideas for using familiar materials. The teacher provides the materials and the focus, but the children are permitted and encouraged to explore and use their own ideas. While teachers have a purpose and a plan for how the group activity may proceed, they allow children to expand their ideas, scaffolding instruction to move children to a higher level when appropriate by building on children's knowledge and discoveries.

Although Small Group Time is teacher initiated, it's important to remember that it involves all the elements of active learning. We should see children manipulating materials in their own ways, experimenting and exploring, with support from the teacher if needed. Interaction between group members is emphasized. The teacher takes a backseat at this time and observes the children. She may occasionally make comments but knows that limited questions while experimentation is happening, is often best.

Small Group Time is not a time for teacher directed lessons, worksheets, coloring sheets, or complicated games.

Small Group Time Step-by-Step

Before:

- Decide the focus of the small group session based on the needs, interests, and developmental levels of the children in the group.
- Gather and prepare materials from the classroom
- Have a set of materials for each child
- Locate any additional materials that may be needed

The Big Idea:

- Read a short section of a book, tell a story, or briefly introduce the activity
- Demonstrate the big idea (whole concept) with the materials
- Children listen and observe
- Get the materials in the children's hands as soon as possible

During Small Group Time:

- Put your set of materials away
- Children "do" under supervision and with support from teacher
- Children experiment with the materials in their own way
- Move to the children—get on their level
- Watch, listen to the children, and observe
- Provide comments and use parallel talk.
- Ask a few open-ended questions for children who are ready to respond, but don't force a question/response dialogue unless children show they are ready
- Respond to children's questions
- Provide the extra materials, if needed.

Wrapping it up:

- Provide a warning that Small Group Time will end soon, but realize that children often finish at different times
- Tell children that they may choose to continue to work with the materials during Work Time, which comes next
- Talk about the Small Group with children while they cleanup
- Have a transition plan to the next segment of the daily routine and allow children to transition as they finish

CIRCLES STRATEGY: Small Group Time

1. **The Big Idea.** Share the big picture idea in words that children can understand. The Big Idea is connected to the goal in your lesson plan and a learning domain.
2. **Model/Demonstrate.** Provide a brief demonstration or model the idea for children. "Do" what you want children to do or learn. Show the whole and then pull the pieces apart. Avoid asking questions at this time, and don't expect questions from them. Simply do, and talk about what you are doing. (self-talk, watch-then-do) While the teacher is doing, the children…
3. **Observe/Listen.** The children observe and carefully, respectfully, listen.
4. Children Do. Children "do" under supervision. Questions and responses are good from both sides. Talk about what children are doing (parallel talk) and encourage discussion if children want. If children do not want to discuss, that is okay (they could be processing and reflecting).
5. **Individual Experimentation.** Continue time for children to experiment with materials without adult supervision.

Small Group Process—Example from the Scenario	
The Big Idea	Both teachers begin their Small Groups by reading a few more pages of Eating the Alphabet. The focus for Miss Sarah's group is to practice identifying and matching upper and lower case letters. Later in the week she will add writing the upper and lower case letters. Mr. Charlie's group will focus on letters too, but his goal is more about manipulating them, than identifying and matching. He has added play dough to his list of materials for the children to use. He wants to help them work on building their fine motor skills, while playing with the letters.
Model/ Demonstrate	After Miss Sarah has read a little more of the story, she puts her book down flat on the table. Then she gets some magnetic letters out of her baggie, and with the children, starts matching the letters to the ones on the pages in the book. She lays an upper case A on top of the upper case A in the book.
Observe/ Listen	She provides several more examples, using self-talk to talk about what she is doing while she is doing it, and while the children watch and listen. "I'm putting this red upper case A on this red upper case A on this page."
Do/Individual Experimenta- tion	Miss Sarah puts her materials away while the children work. She wanted to provide them with the big idea, but she doesn't necessarily want them to copy what she did. She allows them to work and ask questions if they want. She provides support when, and if, needed, but doesn't overpower the conversation at the table with her words. She is more interested in hearing dialogue and conversation from the children, and knows that if all of the airspace is filled with her words, children may feel there is no space left for their words.

Work Time: Wonder-Work-Share

At the end of Small Group Time, Teacher Sarah says, "We'll keep these materials here on the table, and some of you may choose to work with them during Work Time. Okay?"

The children nod. Joe says, "It's Work Time now, Miss Sarah. Right? What are we going to wonder about?"

Teacher Sarah smiles. "That's right, Joe. Will you help me move the marker in a minute?" He nods and heads to the circle. "We might have to ask Mr. Charlie about wondering."

Mr. Charlie says to the children, "Today I was wondering about the snow outside. How long do you think it will be before it melts?" For the next minute or so, while the children gather in the circle, he leads a quick discussion about the melting snow, asking questions like, "What makes the snow melt?" and "Why does the snow get dirty?"

Then Miss Sarah sits down and says, "Time for Wonder!"

She and the children since a short song that she made up about Wonder Time, sung to the tune of Oh My Darling, Clementine.

>"It is Wonder Time. It is Wonder Time. It is Wonder Time today.
>I will think and I will ponder during wonder time today.

>"Use my brain. Use my mind. My imagination too.
>I will think and I will ponder during wonder time with you.

>"I'll be curious. I will marvel. I will ask some questions too.
>I will think and I will ponder during wonder time with you."

>[Repeat first verse]

Miss Sarah has learned that her children need a brief transition activity between Small Group Time and Work Time. The children respond better during work time with a few moments to come back together first. When finished singing the song, she says, "I promised Joe he could move the marker next."

Joe goes to the wall and moves the marker from Small Group Time to the Work Time block. He turns to Miss Sarah. "I know where I want to play today."

"Okay," says Miss Sarah, "I am wondering what you are going to do today. Why don't you tell me in a sentence or two?"

Joe nods. "Today I am going to play in the Block Area."

(continued)

> Miss Sarah nods back. "I wonder what you will do there?"
>
> Joe replies, "I am going to build a train station and I am going to ship the animals from the desert to the zoo!"
>
> Miss Sarah says, "Wow! I wonder what those animals think about that!"
>
> Joe grins and says, "They are wondering if there will be food there."
>
> "Hm," says Miss Sarah. "Food is important. Who else will play with you?"
>
> Joe eagerly nods. "I hope Tate will play in the Block Area too. We can ship the animals together."
>
> Miss Sarah says, "Why don't you go ahead and get started, Joe. Take your Plan Man to the Block Area. You know where it goes," then she turns to Tate. "Tate, Joe says he hopes to play with you today. What do you think about that?"
>
> Teacher Sarah knows that Joe understands how to plan for Work Time, so she attempts to get more questions and sentences from him while he is planning. She also knows that some of her students are not at that high level of planning yet. She and Tate briefly plan, and then she and her co-teacher help the rest of the children plan for Work Time, asking a few more questions and for more words, when appropriate. This takes about five minutes.

Wonder-Work-Share is a key element of the CIRCLES curriculum morning routine. It is the time of day when children "wonder" or intentionally think about and plan their work, and choose in what Learning Area they want to do this work. With support from teachers, children talk about their ideas and the materials they want to work with, what they might do or create, and who they might work with that day. Then, children work and carry out their plans over the next 45-60 minutes. Finally, children are offered an opportunity to share or reflect on the work they did in a large group, thinking again about their plans, and sharing with other children and the teachers. In CIRCLES, we call this process Wonder-Work-Share.

Work Time: Wonder and Planning

As in Teacher Sarah's scenario above, sometimes it is beneficial to bring children together for a brief Wonder Time after Small Group Time, followed by planning for Work Time. As a transition, Miss Sarah's class sang the Wonder Time song.

When a teacher says to a child, "I wonder where you'll work today," she's initiating a planning process where the child is asked to express his intention for Work Time. At first, children may simply point to a work area in the classroom or express their intention with single words such as "blocks" or "paint." With teacher support as the year progresses, children's plans will become increasingly complex. Eventually they will be able to tell teachers where they'd like to play or work, the materials they will use and who they might like to join in play, using complete sentences.

Joe, as do all of the children in Miss Sarah's classroom, uses a Plan Man for planning. A "Plan Man" is a simple cutout shape of a person, like a gingerbread cookie shape, with a picture of Joe's face on the "man's" head. Miss Sarah has laminated each child's Plan Man for durability. The children take their Plan Man to the work area they choose, and put it in a pocket on the side of the shelf in that area. This is one way that the teachers can keep track of which, and how many children, are in each area. Also, it helps children to make a plan, and to be redirected to that plan, or provide a chance to change their plan.

> **Planning helps provide children with a focus—to think about what they want to do, to say it aloud, and to actually do it.**

There are many devices to use for planning, and often times teachers will develop their own ideas. A planning board works well for some classrooms. Some teachers use objects like microphones or binoculars to share their plans. Whatever method used, the important thing is that children plan, and communicate that plan with the teacher. Simple planning ideas are best at the beginning of the year, and can get more complicated as the children grow more comfortable with detailed plans.

Planning helps provide children with a focus—to think about what they want to do, to say it aloud, and to actually do it. Later on, at the end of Work Time, children will reflect on their plan.

Once all of the children settle into a learning area, Miss Sarah and her co-teacher, Mr. Charlie, observe the children and enter into their play for support when needed. They jot down some of their observations on note cards when they can, which is part of their informal assessment process. They know that children need time to get into play and work together, so they do not interfere with their play too quickly. When they do, they observe for a moment to understand what is going on, lend some support with an idea, or scaffold with new language, and then step back to see how children take the support and move it forward. Teachers sit on the floor with the children but do not take over children's play. They are there, of course, for helping children to problem solve, but they also know that part of social development, is helping children learn to solve problems or issues during play on their own.

Miss Sarah loves when the classroom is busy and noisy during Work Time. She always says, "Learning isn't always quiet!" In fact, sometimes it can be loud. She scans the room and sees two children making messy art projects with glue, construction paper, paint, and pipe cleaners in the art area. Over in the House Area, three girls and one boy are playing restaurant—flipping pizza crusts and taking orders, setting the table and quieting crying baby dolls. In the Block Area, Joe and Tate are joined by Serena. The zoo animals are herded into a corral while the train track to the zoo is still under construction. Over in the Writing Area, one child uses stampers and stencils to make some letter designs on white paper, while looking at an Eating the Alphabet book. Next to that area, another child is working on Starfall.com on the computer, and Mr. Charlie is adding some support. As Miss Sarah continues to scan the room, she sees children playing with puppets and books in the Book Area, and hears loud voices and the clanging of symbols coming from the music shelf across the room. She heads that way....

Teacher Sarah knows that learning can sometimes be messy, too, which is why she and Mr. Charlie have a system worked out for cleaning up after Work Time. The children know this system, too.

After almost 50 minutes of Work Time, Miss Sarah sets a timer and says to the children, "We have five minutes to finish our work before cleanup. Joe, will you remind me when this timer goes off? That means it's cleanup time."

"Yes, Miss Sarah!" Joe glances to the kitchen timer while he and Tate work on getting the animals in the zoo. Finally, the timer goes off and Joe says, "Miss Sarah! It's cleanup time!"

She smiles and reaches for the timer. "Mr. Charlie, should we put on the cleanup song?" He puts a CD in the player—it's the same cleanup song they play every day. When children hear that song, they know what to do next. (Some, of course, a little slower than others.)

> Clean-up time takes about another five minutes. Sometimes when the children are slower at cleanup, she sets the timer again, or challenges them to a game of getting cleaned up, "before the cleanup song ends." This gives children an endpoint for cleanup, so they can keep on schedule and move on to the next block in their daily routine.

Work Time: *Work*

As children go to the work areas of the classroom, they will be carrying out their stated plans by working/playing, doing and learning. They will manipulate materials, make choices, and use their imaginations. They may work by themselves or with others but always will be actively engaged with their own ideas, creating, making decisions, solving problems, and constructing their own knowledge through their experiences. During Work Time it is likely that children will move about the classroom, working in several areas on several projects and with a variety of classmates. Even though children have made initial plans at the beginning of Work Time, it is okay for children to change their plans, clean up, and move to another work area, as long as the area is not too crowded, or one child is not infringing upon another child's play. Each teacher will set the boundaries and barriers about work areas so that all children understand how Work time "works" best in the classroom.

The teacher's role during Work Time is to observe what children are doing, learn about their interests and abilities, and support their work/play to maximize learning outcomes. Throughout Work Time, teachers will engage with children, respectfully entering their play to participate at their physical level and talk with them about what they are doing. Teachers may provide additional materials to extend children's play and thinking, may extend children's language and vocabulary, or may help groups solve problems.

> **The teacher's role during Work Time is to observe what children are doing, learn about their interests and abilities, and support their work/play.**

Work Time is a child-led time of the day, and not a time for teachers to set up stations or centers, with planned activities for children to do. It is not a time for worksheets or guided play. Work Time is the time for children to create their own play, carry out their own plans, explore, experiment, and learn. When children finish work time and clean up, then everyone comes back together to reflect on their hour of work.

"Remember, as soon as your area is cleaned up, let's come together in the circle area." Mr. Charlie is leading the review part of Work Time today."

Most of the children head to the circle. Some are still cleaning up under Miss Sarah's supervision.

"Wow. We had a good Work Time today," Mr. Charlie says. "Let's all think about what we did today at Work Time while everyone is gathering together."

When all children are ready, Miss Sarah says, "I wonder what everyone did today?"

Mr. Charlie leads a 5 to 10-minute share/reflect session. Today he has decided to pick up a few items from the environment he saw children working with. He puts them in a mystery bag and the children guess what he might pull out. One-by-one he pulls out objects saying, "I wonder who played with this! If you played with a paint brush today, raise your hand." Then Mr. Charlie lets each child tell in a sentence what he or she did with the paintbrush. When choosing objects, Mr. Charlie tries to choose items that several children played with that day, so the review goes more quickly. His goal is for each child to say a sentence telling about that object. "Today I played with dolls." He helps some children extend the discussion. "Today I played with dolls and I took them to the doctor." For the older children, Mr. Charlie may try to get more words from them. "What happened at the doctor?"

Some children, Mr. Charlie knows, are not yet ready to share. He doesn't push them and lets them think about their play. Soon, he knows, they will want to share too, and he'll start to expand their conversations then.

When Mr. Charlie finishes, Miss Sarah says, "I'm thinking about the letters we worked with in Small Group today, and the book we read at Circle Time. Remember?" She holds up the book, Eating the Alphabet. "We're going to be working with this book more this week. Did anyone work with the letters at Work Time today. Jamie? Did I see you at the Small Group table?"

Jamie smiles and nods his head.

"Do you have anything you want to say about the letters?"

He grins. "They matched."

"That's right! I saw you matching letters today. Anything else you want to share?"

He shakes his head no, and Miss Sarah says, "That's okay. Anyone else have anything to say about the letters?"

> None of the children respond immediately so Miss Sarah gives a brief moment of silence to let them think, then moves on. She knows they will be working with the letters often, and will come back to them soon. Together, she and Mr. Charlie spend about 10 minutes on share/reflect today.

Work Time: *Share/Reflect*

Share/reflect is a time where children think about the work they just did. About an hour earlier, they planned, and now it is time to share and reflect. It is important that this reflection time comes as close to work time as possible, so be sure to schedule it before lunch, and not after.

Once the children have cleaned up the materials, they come back together in the circle to reflect what they did during Work Time, and to share how they carried out their initial plans. This is an opportunity for children to connect their plans to their work, and to reflect on their actions. Children's ability to reflect and evaluate their experiences becomes more thoughtful over time with support from adults. They also develop skills in communicating their experiences effectively to others.

The ability to reflect or recall an experience is a cognitive learning activity.

Being able to reflect, or recall, an experience is a cognitive learning activity. Being able to recall and talk about the experience, also supports language and literacy development, and is related to reading comprehension.

Coming full circle. Notice that Teacher Sarah comes full circle back to the Big Idea subject she introduced at Circle Time this morning. By beginning and ending the children's morning with the main focus of the day, she is helping them to be more cognizant of the learning taking place. Today she did the following:

- Gave a global, *visual view* of the Big Idea by introducing and reading the *Eating the Alphabet* book to children during Circle Time, and by coming back to it again at the beginning of Small Group Time.
- In Small Group, she *demonstrated* what she wanted children to do with the *Eating the Alphabet* book, and the magnetic letters, while they *observed and listened*.
- Also in Small Group, the children were provided the books and letters, and they proceeded to *do* what the teacher did, in their own ways, under teacher supervision. Miss Sarah supported their *doing* by using comments and parallel talk, but not by asking a lot of quizzing questions. She let children know that they can experiment with the materials any way they like.
- In Work Time, the alphabet materials and books were left on the Small Group table, so children could continue to work and *experiment* with them on their own, if they chose.
- At the end of Work Time, during share/reflection, Miss Sarah purposely returned to talk about the books and letters. She specifically observed during Work Time if any children did return to the letters after Small Group, so she could *reflect* with the children specifically.

> When Mr. Charlie is finished with share/reflect time, Miss Sarah, still sitting on the floor, says to the children. "Well, Wonder-Work-Share is over for today. What's next?"
>
> "Lunch!" Everyone always knows when it's time for lunch. Miss Sarah says, "That's right," and both teachers transition their children into washing their hands and getting ready for lunch. During this transition time, Mr. Charlie plays a Simon Says game with the children who are waiting, and Miss Sarah supervises the restroom while children are washing up. They sing the "Row, Row, Row Your Boat" song while washing hands, and talk about killing germs. The children line up, and walk to the cafeteria, where some of their parents are waiting.

Meal and Snack Times

Most preschool programs offer meals or snacks as part of their daily routine. Instead of viewing these times as just one more responsibility for the teachers, mealtimes can be seen as valuable learning experience for children. Mealtime routines can teach children responsibility and independence and can support their developing social, academic and language skills.

Ideally, meals and snacks should be served at tables where small groups of children can sit and converse with each other, and with at least one adult. Before mealtime, children can assist in cleaning and setting the tables. Math skills can be reinforced as helpers count the number of plates needed and match napkins and cups one-to-one. All children wash their hands before taking their places at the tables.

When possible, have children serve themselves at mealtime. Passing plates or bowls, serving food and pouring drinks are important motor skills and develop self-confidence and independence. Engage children in conversation, encouraging them to share experiences, express ideas and listen to each other. Build children's oral language by introducing new vocabulary, occasionally asking open-ended questions and expanding on what they say. Reinforce basic table manners like sitting in their chairs, using their napkins, and asking politely for food or drink.

Family-type meal settings, however, cannot happen in the majority of classrooms in American Indian schools. Most children in American Indian programs move to the school cafeteria for lunch. This type of situation is also more accommodating for parents who come to school for lunch, considering space and seating options.

When possible, especially for snack time, include foods that are familiar to children—dishes that represent their culture and homes so that conversations can be based on shared experiences. Most American Indian schools and programs, however, rely on the Federal Lunch program guidelines for meals and snacks, so although ideal, providing culturally relevant foods is not always possible.

The majority of American Indian preschool children qualify for the Federal Lunch program, and receive breakfast, snack, and lunch when coming to school.

Outdoor Time

Outdoor Time is an important part of the daily routine and essential to the preschool curriculum. The outdoor learning environment is viewed as an extension of the preschool classroom. Outdoor learning spaces can be designed to support a wide range of activities and developmental areas. For example, in addition to the standard playground equipment for preschoolers (slides, swings, climbing apparatus, etc.) we might see areas for the following: sandbox, water, wheeled toys, construction, woodworking, garden, ball area, etc. Materials from the classroom can be brought outdoors as well for children to experience in new and imaginative ways. With a little preparation and creative management, dramatic play, blocks, music & movement, play dough and paints can all be used effectively outdoors. Teachers can also look for natural opportunities for discovery and science. With a little support, children will notice and explore the insects, animals, plants, mud and other natural materials in your outdoor environment.

Adequate outdoor time each day in a creatively designed environment provides unique opportunities for supporting the development of children's skills in several domains of the Early Childhood Standards:

Physical Development: As children engage regularly in noisy, active, outdoor play they naturally have opportunities to develop skills in many of the Physical Development standards:

- Gross Motor
- Fine Motor
- Sensory
- Safety

Parent and Child Together (PACT) Time®

> Sometimes parents arrive for lunch and stay for PACT Time, which happens in the afternoon. After lunch, children participate in a 15-minute recess or gross motor time outside. Parents accompany them and help support their play. While they are walking back to the classroom from the playground, Miss Sarah asks the children to think about what they want to do with their parents today during PACT Time. Children share their play ideas with their parents.
>
> "Clara, what work do you want to do with your mother today at PACT Time? Why don't you share with her?"
>
> Clara looks up at Miss Sarah. "Letters and play dough," she says.
>
> Miss Sarah adds, "Why don't you tell you mom and say it in a sentence. Okay?"
>
> Clara nods and turns to her mom. "I want to play with letters and play dough today."
>
> Clara's mom says, "Okay! Do you have ideas?"
>
> Smiling, Clara nods. "Yes!"
>
> Once they return to the classroom, a PACT Time session begins. Parents follow their children's lead and support their play. These PACT Time sessions can vary from day to day, and look different from program to program.
>
> While some children have parents in the classroom, children like Joe do not. Miss Sarah and Mr. Charlie make sure those children get attention from the two of them. PACT Time is a lot like Work Time, but a bit shorter—maybe 30-40 minutes total, depending on each classroom's schedule. At the end of PACT Time, all children and parents clean up the work areas together while talking (reflecting) about what they did that day. Then they come together for a brief closing Circle Time—usually reading a book, or singing a song together—and the teachers provide a Transfer Home idea for parents and children to take home and do together later.

***Wonder-Work-Share* in PACT Time**

The *Wonder-Work-Share* sequence discussed early in Work Time is also used during PACT Time. Parents are informed of the value of children developing confidence and initiative around their work and play and are supported in implementing these strategies during PACT Time. Rather than a sharing in a group, parents are encouraged to review and reflect with their children as they bring their PACT activity to a close and clean up. As parents become comfortable allowing their children to make choices and following their children's lead in play, they come to appreciate the benefits and often think of ways to use this same approach at home.

Preschool programs with a family learning focus take advantage of having both parents and children on site. This opportunity can enhance connections, allow parents to practice new skills, and increase the likelihood of timely and effective review and reflection. This center-based model of parent-child interaction is often seen in preschools connected to family literacy/family learning programs, and has been an integral part of parent engagement offered in American Indian programs like the Family and Child Education (FACE) program.

In a center-based preschool/family education program, PACT Time generally happens in the following sequence:

- *Parents Prepare with Support from Staff.* Staff and parents discuss a number of different ideas for interactions and decide on one that reflects the child's interests, developmental goals, and the parents' interests in support their child's language and literacy development.

- *Parents and Children Plan Together.* Parents and children discuss where to work or play, what they will do together, what materials they may use, and what they might talk about during the interaction.

- *Parents and Children Work and Play Together.* Parents engage with their children and respond to their child's lead. They act as models for their children, utilizing new strategies learned from parent education, or previous parent-child interactions. Staff act as a participant observer, providing materials when necessary, watching for the strengths of the interaction. When appropriate, staff also join in the play and act as models for parent and child. This is an opportunity for joint interactions between staff, parents and children—an open and relaxed chance for interaction and fun.

- *Parents and Children Review.* Parents and children have a simple conversation about their work and play as they clean up, encouraging a habit of review and reflection.

- *Parents and Children Participate in Circle Time.* This time is an opportunity for parents and children to come together in a large group experience for a literacy activity. Often this will be a Circle Time activity that involves reading a book, participating in a game, song or finger play, and concluding with an idea to transfer the learning home. This Transfer Home activity will reinforce the learning that happened in the classroom, and is intentionally planned and designed to meet children's goals for language and literacy development.

- *Parents Review/Reflect.* Reflection time is most effective when it happens soon after PACT Time. Parents may discuss or write in a journal their reflections of their children's learning and their time together, often internalizing new understandings and strategies. The setting for the reflection varies depending on program design, but is often done at the beginning of a parent education session. Some review opportunities may be brief, while others may be more detailed and lengthy. This time is a natural opportunity to discuss children and their growth. This review and reflection time guides parents in thinking about the next interactive experience they will have with their child.

> **Preschool programs with a family learning focus take advantage of having both parents and children on site.**

Rest/Quiet Time and Departure

> As the children transition from PACT Time to rest time, parents leave the classroom. Some stay to help Mr. Charlie and Miss Sarah get the cots in place. Joe knows his pillow and blanket are located in his cubby and rushes to get it. "May I have a quiet toy too?" he asks.
>
> Miss Sarah nods and says, "Yes," then begins to lower the shades. "All of my friends need their pillows and blankets. Please find your cot. And if you need a quiet toy, like Joe, you may get one from the quiet toy box."
>
> While the children snuggle into their cots for rest time, Miss Sarah reads to them in a soft, low voice. Mr. Charlie quietly works on straightening toys and checks the lesson plan book to pull the materials for tomorrow's Small Group. While the children rest, Miss Sarah and Mr. Charlie quietly discuss lesson plans, file their observation notes, or review children's files. They take advantage of a few moments of quiet time to prepare for the next day, make plans for screenings and assessments, and other teacher tasks.
>
> Joe's mom arrives a little early as the children begin to wake and move around. She asks Miss Sarah if it's okay to read another story to Joe while the children are preparing for home. Miss Sarah smiles and says, "Of course."
>
> "Hi Mom." Joe sits up and lifts up a book. "I got the zoo book. Read it again?" Her heart swells as she sits on the floor next to him and quietly reads. She notices other parents arriving and some children leaving, but she is content to spend a little quiet time with Joe before they go. Things will get hectic as soon as they get home, she knows—dinner, baths, homework for the older children— she's happy for this time alone with him.

Rest/Quiet Time is an important part of the day for many preschoolers. We prefer using the terms "rest" or "quiet", instead of "nap." We want this to be a pleasant time for children, and many young children associate the term "nap" with a negative time of the day. In addition, older children may have outgrown a nap time and will not sleep—but they can come to enjoy some quiet time to wind down and play quietly while others are sleeping.

Young children need rest in order to do their best in school. Typically, rest time is after lunch and classrooms are equipped with cots, blankets and pillows for every child. Children should have an established spot for resting and a regular routine should be in place to help them feel secure.

When the classroom lights are dimmed, soft music plays in the background, and snuggling with a favorite stuffed toy or blanket is permitted. Children typically welcome this opportunity to take a break from their busy day—but teachers will need a plan for children who do not sleep or who wake up early. Have a selection of books or quiet toys available to engage those children so as not to disturb the rest of the group. Plan a flexible activity following rest time—such as a time for child choice of play—so children can wake up on their own schedule and easily rejoin the larger group.

Many teachers read quietly to children during rest time. Not all children will sleep, but they must lay quiet and rest so that others can sleep. Reading a few stories aloud for children helps keep consistency and the resting children engaged. Don't be concerned about asking questions as this time. Reading at rest time is not the time for engagement or dialogic reading strategies. It is a pleasant time for children to listen and calm themselves for a few minutes, by listening to the soft and rhythmic cadence of reading.

Many of the younger children may sleep until their parents arrive and it is time to depart. Gauge whether this is okay by how the parents feel about children sleeping late. Some won't mind, and others may worry about getting children to bed on time later that evening. Some children simply need the rest, or may not be feeling well. Use your best judgement and talk with parents to get their input.

Some teachers plan a closing circle at the end of the day, but others find it difficult to get all children awake and alert enough to enjoy listening to a book or singing a song. If a closing Circle Time becomes more chaotic, than beneficial, it is okay to skip it and let children move into the rest of the day with their parents naturally.

Miss Sarah glances back from the door where she has been saying good-bye to a few children and parents. Mr. Charlie has already led the bus riders down the hallway. She smiles, watching Joe and his mom enjoy the book together before they go home.

With a deep and satisfying sigh, she heads to her lesson plan book where she will go over today's lessons and make some notes. Once Mr. Charlie comes back to the classroom, they will reflect and discuss the day's activities together, decide what adjustments to make in their lesson plans for tomorrow, and plan accordingly.

Handling transitions during the day

Preschool classrooms are full of *in-between* times, commonly called transitions. Children arrive, depart, clean up, get ready for snack, greet parents, leave parents, and enter into and out of play and activities all day long. Sometimes children react strongly to such changes making transitions difficult for children, parents and teachers. However, transitions don't have to be chaotic. With appropriate planning and supportive strategies, transitions can provide intentional opportunities for learning new concepts and reinforcing skills in the preschool classroom.

Transitions and daily routines go hand-in-hand. As children move throughout their day, the time they experience between activities becomes valuable. It's been said that as much as 15% of a child's day is spent in transition. Strive for as few transitions as possible, especially when parents are involved. Move transitions along quickly and always have a plan for how to make the transition a smooth one. Maximizing transition times can provide optimal impact for children.

Some guidelines for planning and using transitions:

Use transition activities while you:

- gather children in small or large groups
- move children from one location to another
- fill in short gaps of time between activities
- focus children's attention

Transitions should:

- keep children actively engaged
- provide a natural flow from one activity to the next
- complement a predictable, consistent daily routine
- include a balance of active and quiet activities
- include children's ideas and interests
- be fun and quick
- be intentional and planned
- provide a change of pace in the routine

Teachers should:

- minimize children's waiting time
- make children aware of upcoming transitions (provide a warning)
- use a variety of transition activities

- avoid moving large groups of children at once
- allow sufficient time for the transition
- involve children by assigning tasks
- provide clear instruction
- be flexible
- be prepared
- minimize the number of transitions during the day where parents arrive and leave the classroom

In the preschool classroom:

- have a notebook or card file of transition ideas handy
- use rhymes, poems, finger plays and songs
- use games, riddles and movement
- use props such as scarves, hoops, carpet squares, flashlights, puppets, etc. to engage children and grab their attention
- use transitions to get jobs done, i.e., daily sign-in, preparing for snack, cleanup, introducing new materials in centers, preparing for naps, etc.
- make the educational

Some more Daily Routine ideas for teachers—at the beginning of the year

The basic daily routine for your classroom should be in place on the first day of school. We want children to learn the routine as soon as possible and to feel secure in its predictability. Have a visual representation posted and refer to the elements of the routine as the day progresses. Although time allotments may be adjusted at the beginning of the year, the daily activities should all be in place.

As the year begins, your morning *Circle Time* should be fairly short, active, and engaging to respond to young children's limited attention span. The use of big books that everyone can see will engage children in stories during Circle Time. Teachers can use basic interactive reading strategies right away, including reading expressively and asking simple questions to support listening and promote discussion. Finger plays and songs with movements also encourage participation in active ways.

Small Group Time in the first part of the year can be used to introduce children to the materials that are available throughout the classroom. Plan open-ended activities by bringing materials from one of the interest areas and encouraging children's exploration and experimentation. Facilitate discussion among the children and support problem-solving as challenges arise.

For example, bring play dough from the Art Area and a set of cookie cutters or other tools. Use the materials yourself and model the use of devices that are not familiar to the children. Or bring a supply of Duplo blocks to the table or simple puzzles or watercolor paints. This is a perfect opportunity to be sure children are aware of materials that are available in the classroom and understand their use. At the end of small group, leave the materials on the table and remind children they can explore further during Work Time. Be flexible with the amount of time allocated for Small Group at the beginning of the year and be ready to transition as interest fades.

As children will be naturally interested in exploring their new classroom, **Work Time** may be the largest block of time in the daily routine during the first few months of the year. Introduce the **Wonder-Work-Share** process from the start by using simple planning and sharing strategies. A planning board with photographs of each interest area can facilitate children's responses to "I wonder where you will work today…" by reminding them of their choices. During Work Time, both teachers will be actively engaged with children in the interest areas, offering support when needed, facilitating conversation and teaching about managing and cleaning up toys and materials. After Work Time, teachers can help children share by revisiting the interest area photographs and asking, "Who played here today?" or bringing actual materials used in the work areas to the circle for children to share.

Planning and sharing at the beginning of the year will be simple, but it's important to introduce the process from the start.

Daily Routine Checklist

This checklist represents the kinds of best practices often seen in high quality early childhood classrooms relating to children's daily routines. The checklist encompasses all children including those with disabilities, learning styles, and dual language learners (DLL). Indicate your level of practices in these areas below.

A daily routine supports preschool children's growth, development, and learning. Is each item below routine practice for you, or an area of improvement?	Routine Practice	Area of Improvement
Provide clearly defined routines with a schedule posted at children's eye-level.		
Post daily routine schedule in left-to-right order to help children develop left-to-right progression needed for reading.		
Use clear pictures or icons on the daily schedule at the beginning of the year. Add words later for children to begin relating print to concepts. (Times are not needed for preschoolers.)		
Post a linear schedule with times of day at adult eye-level for parents and other visitors. This could be inside, or just outside of the classroom.		
Plan for extended arrival/departure times with intentional activities for parents and children during staggered arrivals and departures.		
Plan for a balance of quiet (rest) and active times throughout the day.		
Provide for smooth transitions between activities. No wasted time.		
Plan a balance of large group, small group, and individual work times for children throughout the day.		
Plan for a balance of experiences that address all domains of learning—social/emotional, physical (gross and fine motor), and academic (math, science, language, literacy, social studies), and creative arts.		
Provide at least one hour of child planned/initiated work time within the daily routine.		
Allow time for children to experiment and reflect before responding. Be culturally responsive and wait for verbal responses.		
Provide times for children to choose to read alone or look at books. (Transitions, Rest Time, Work Time, Arrival/Departure)		
Plan to read aloud to children 3-7 times during the day. Indicate the time of day in lesson plans.		
When parents come for PACT Time: • Minimize transitions by careful placement of when PACT Time happens throughout the day. • Plan for a brief PACT Time Circle each day for parents/children to reflect and share with each other. • Provide a transfer-home activity for parents and children with each PACT Time experience at school.		
Use responsive adult-child interactive strategies to model good oral language practices with children throughout the day.		
Utilize a consistent but flexible daily routine where children feel secure and can predict what comes next in their day.		

Planning for Children

How do I know what to teach?
By finding out what children know and can do through observation and ongoing assessment.

Assessment to Instruction

Assessing children's development and learning is essential in the CIRCLES® Curriculum. The assessment process provides teachers with information about children and guides the development of appropriate lesson planning and instruction that promotes the "next steps" in children's learning.

Assessing children's abilities, developing appropriate curriculum, and planning for daily instruction are all part of the assessment to instruction process. Assessment is essential to curriculum and provides a basis for planning instruction, communicating with parents, identifying children's needs and goals, and evaluating program impact.

Let's define some of the terms we will use in this section.

Screening: A stand-alone process or instrument, often a one-time occurrence that is conducted soon after the child enrolls in school. Screening is a first step in identifying children in need of further assessment. The process reviews multiple sources of information and determines students' strengths and areas for improvement.

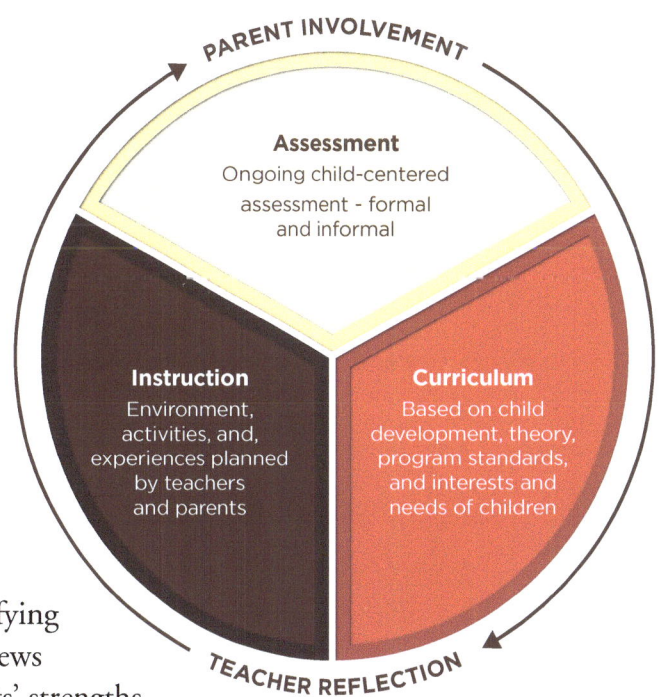

103

Assessment: The ongoing process of observing, recording and documenting the work children do and how they do it. Assessment is a collection of information on children's abilities to determine progress, identify areas for intervention, plan instruction, and make educational decisions. A variety of sources may be used to gather information. Assessment is used for planning for individual children and communicating with parents, and to determine whether instructional strategies or a program is working. Assessment can be authentic (or informal) or formal. See the definitions that follow.

Authentic (informal) assessments are part of an ongoing process of documentation and evaluation designed to inform instructional practices. These assessments are usually based on observation, anecdotal notes, samples of children's work, developmental checklists, and parent and teacher report. Authentic assessments are collected in a variety of ways over time.

Formal assessments are norm-referenced, standardized, and/or criterion-referenced instruments that produce a score to compare with other students or criteria. They often require administration by someone who has been trained or has the qualifications to administer the test.

Curriculum

The CIRCLES® Program Framework lays the foundational groundwork for teaching and learning. It addresses how the *child learns and is taught* within his or her own *home, school,* and *community*. It takes into consideration children's unique approaches to learning and their preferred learning styles. This foundational framework is the result of evidence-based practice.

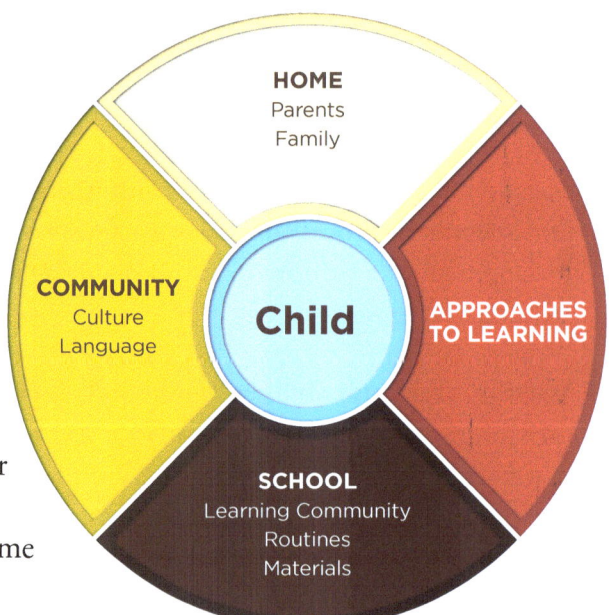

In this framework children are at the center of their learning. We know that children learn best within learning communities that are inclusive of their home culture, their Native language, and their families.

Teachers build the curriculum for children week by week, by creating lesson plans for children based on:

- *what they know about their students,*
- *their observation of students and their work,*
- *what they learn about students from ongoing assessment, and*
- *what parents tell teachers about their children.*

Ongoing assessment includes authentic assessment methods, such as observation, collecting work samples, and developmental checklists.

Teachers facilitate and individualize children's learning throughout the instructional day by adapting classroom routines, materials, and strategies to meet children's needs to meet their developmental goals.

Why do we build the curriculum week by week? Because three- and four-year old children grow and develop rapidly over these two years. Young children are also individuals who have differing needs. Their development varies from child to child. Often children require individualized instruction that cannot be met by a standardized, cookie-cutter approach to teaching. This curriculum approach is created out of the current needs of the children in the classroom—from paying close attention to where children are developmentally and where they need to go next, and planning instruction accordingly.

Preschool classrooms frequently have multiple levels of learners in one classroom, aging from three- to five years of age. This requires a flexible approach to curriculum and the ability to individualize for all children per their abilities and learning goals.

The CIRCLES Early Childhood Learning Domains—3-5 Years, provide the benchmarks for what children should know and be able to do by kindergarten entry. In the CIRCLES Curriculum, these Learning Domains are used like standards to plan lesson plans. Programs using existing state or program level standards can easily substitute those standards in the CIRCLES Curriculum for planning instruction.

See the **CIRCLES Early Childhood Learning Domains—3-5 Years** provided later in this chapter.

Instruction

Once teachers have identified learning goals and areas of focus that are appropriate for their preschool students based on their observations and assessment data, they will choose materials, design lessons, and plan interactions and experiences for the week that will address those learning goals.

The **CIRCLES® Learning Framework** focuses on specific teaching strategies. Teachers use this strategy within the morning routine, particularly in Circle Time, Small Group Time, and Work Time. The CIRCLES® Learning Framework is based on learning styles relevant to American Indian learners and supports children's individual approaches to learning.

Using the **CIRCLES® Daily Lesson Plan**, teachers plan daily lesson plans for children that directly connect to the Learning Domains (or standards), and are designed to help children reach kindergarten ready goals.

Teacher Reflection

Besides being diligent observers of children, CIRCLES teachers constantly reflect on their lesson plans and the experiences provided to children. What worked? What didn't? Which children need more time with a skill development activity, or with certain materials?

Following instruction, teachers assess children's mastery of the learning goal and make decisions about where to go next with curriculum and instruction. Do children need more time and practice to master this concept? Is it time to move on to another curriculum domain and another learning goal? This constant practice of moving from assessment to instruction and back to assessment again represents the ongoing cycle of assessment-to-instruction.

Taking time to reflect daily, and to write down those reflections on your lesson plan, helps guide how you will build your next week's curriculum—or lesson plans—based upon what you learned about children this week.

Find a weekly time to plan together, teacher and co-teacher. During this planning time

- *reflect* on the past week and make notes in your lesson plan
- *review* children's anecdotal notes and work samples for the week
- *review* any assessment data collected this week
- *plan* the experiences that children need next to scaffold and move learning forward.

Parent Involvement

Parent input regarding children's assessment is vitally important. Parents, as their children's first teachers, know the most about their children. Invite parents to be part of the screening processes so that you can get parent input during the screening. There are several screening measures, such as the Ages and Stages Questionnaire, which invite parent participation to the screening process. Ask parents to complete health information when children are enrolled in school to provide you with some initial insight to the child's general health and well-being.

At least once each semester, set aside a time to meet with parents, discuss children's progress, and set goals for children for the next part of the year. Be sure to include parents in any transition process with children, as they move into and out of the programs—particularly for kindergarten transition.

Referrals

Preschool is a time to screen and assess children not only for the development of lesson plans and curriculum, but to determine if a child may need additional support services provided by the school, the community, or the tribe.

Most school systems and early childhood programs have processes in place to make referrals for children with special needs. Preschool teachers who are unfamiliar with these processes should contact their school administration to learn the local processes and procedures for referring a child for early intervention services. Depending on whether your school is funded by the Department of Education, the Bureau of Indian Education, Head Start, or another early childhood agency, the processes and the agencies to contact may differ.

Most importantly, teachers should know and understand the process, which may look similar to this:

- Conduct a developmental screening
- Review the child's records, including health records
- Talk to parents and learn about the child's health history, growth, and development
- Observe children daily and record anecdotal notes
- Conduct routine assessments, such as a language test, developmental checklists, collect work samples, and formal assessments
- Review all data ongoing
- If child appears to be functioning at a level different than expected for preschoolers, play close attention to observations and anecdotal notes, document behaviors or incidents, and perhaps re-screen the child in areas of concern in a few weeks.
- When screening and formal assessment data indicate concerns, be sure to follow the local protocol for speaking with parents, getting parents to sign off on the referral, and making the referral to the appropriate agency.
- Keep accurate and detailed records and follow-up in a timely manner.
- If it is recommended that a referred child begin an Individualized Education Program (IEP) then the teacher and parent will be a part of this team to determine the educational plan for the child. This plan is then reflected in the teacher's lesson plans.

Observation

Observation is a personal, one-on-one, way of assessing how much a child knows, or what he or she can do. Observation happens over time, and the recorded notes that come from observation can show a child's growth (or lack thereof) over time.

Observation provides teachers the opportunity to slow down and focus on one child—to really watch and observe the struggles a child has, or how they successfully complete a task.

Observation allows teachers to hook into the unique strengths, temperament, learning styles, and individual approaches to learning of children.

Observation allows teachers to connect with children in a way that no formal, standardized, and norm-referenced test can do.

Why do we observe children?
- **To understand a child's strengths, interests, and needs**
- **To understand an individual child's skill development**
- **To plan and implement appropriate learning experiences**
- **To identify areas for early intervention**
- **To document changes in growth, learning, and development over time**
- **To provide a way to talk with parents about children's progress and development**

Writing Anecdotal Observations

Anecdotal notes are the notes you take when you observe children. These notes are important for documenting children's progress.

Writing anecdotal notes of your observations of children shows change and development over time. This type of authentic assessment is based on real performance of the individual child, not an artificial testing situation. Observation provides essential, daily information teachers can use when planning for the coming week.

Teachers use various tools, such as sticky notes and note cards, for recording anecdotal notes. CIRCLES teachers also have the option of using the Recording Anecdotal Notes form that follows this section. This form can slip easily into a clipboard, or can be cut apart into smaller notes. The form allows space to take notes for several children on one page.

Whatever system a teacher uses for writing and collecting anecdotal notes, be sure to include the following information on each note:

- Date
- Child's name
- Time/Section of day (Circle Time, Work Time, Small Group, etc.)

Provide enough information to be able to refer to later:

- Wh's – where, when, who, why
- What happened?
- Write child's speech in quotations to signify the exact words the child said

Write the facts and avoid providing your opinion of what is happening. Notes are written objectively, not subjectively. Give enough information and paint a picture so later you'll remember what you observed. Be brief but meaningful. Use shorthand when possible, for example, Work Time (WT), Circle Time (CT), House Area (HA), etc.

Develop a system of collecting anecdotal notes that works for you and your staff. Plan the times you will observe and record notes. Work Time is a great time to observe children and record your observations. All teachers in the room can and should write and collect anecdotal notes, but may do so at different times. Above all, be consistent and thorough.

By collecting notes over time, teachers are creating an ongoing record of each individual child's abilities, and where they need support. Anecdotal notes help provide documentation for children's growth and development over time and are valuable information to share with parents. Anecdotal notes should be reviewed weekly during lesson planning.

Recording and Using Anecdotal Notes:

- Spend time observing children the first few days of school without writing notes. Get to know their preferences, habits, temperaments, and abilities.
- Set aside times in your lesson plans to record notes. Perhaps indicate a time of day with a *star* or highlight the time you want to capture some observations.
- Be ready to write notes at any time. Sometimes exciting things happen with children when you least expect them. Have your notes or clipboard handy to jot down notes as you can capture them.
- If your clipboard isn't handy but your camera is, snap a quick picture and jot a note to go with it. You can elaborate later when you have a few minutes. Having a digital camera or cell phone camera within reach can be an asset to record the experience digitally (either a still photo or video!). Don't forgot to download and attach the digital experience to the dated anecdotal note.
- Have a system prepared to store the notes, either in hard copy form or online. Perhaps

keep hard copy notes in each child's folder, or set up a filing system specifically for storing notes. Explore digital online or cloud-based systems for storing and sharing notes with your co-teacher or with parents.
- At the end of the week, collect all of the notes written by teachers and bring to your lesson planning meeting. Discuss the observations and categorize them by Learning Domain.
    o   Where are children exhibiting the most skills?
    o   What experiences do you need to provide for children in other domains?
    o   With which materials are children playing with the most? The least?
    o   Where do you need to provide additional supports or materials?
- Keep all anecdotal notes organized to refer to when completing developmental checklists. Use anecdotal notes to make decisions about whether children are just *beginning* a skill, whether the skill is *emerging*, or whether the child is *proficient* or has mastered, a skill.

Collecting Work Samples

Along with writing down notes documenting your observations, collect various samples of children's work to help assess where children are developmentally. These samples of work could be many things, such as:

- Pictures you may take of children's work, or of children working individually or cooperatively with others.
    o   Take pictures of work that may disappear in time, such as a tower a child built, or a painting they want to take home to a family member.
    o   Take action pictures of children participating in large group activities, such as dancing or dramatic play—or pictures of a child doing something they have never done before.
    o   Remember to take pictures of work that is memorable, such as the first time a child put a puzzle together, or the excitement on a child's face when he counted to 10 all by himself.
    o   Pair pictures with anecdotal notes to make your observations richer with the experience and the accomplishment.
- The actual work created, such as a drawing, an art project, a writing sample, a clay figure, or other physical object that represents a child's work and a milestone event.
- Records of children signing in to school each day. A notebook filled with pages of children's daily sign-in sheets can provide documented evidence of a child's progression in writing her name.

Create a method of storing children's work samples for the week, using them to help plan your next week's lesson plans, then return them to children. Remember, you can always take pictures of work samples for your children's portfolios.

Lesson Planning in CIRCLES®

In the CIRCLES® curriculum approach, teachers develop ***weekly lessons plans*** to reflect children's strengths, needs, interests and goals. These lesson plans also document how the standards are directly connected to these goals for children. Use your observations of children, and the information you gain from screenings and assessments, as well as input from parents, to create your goals for children and plan experiences to help them reach these goals.

Each weekly lesson plan is guided by the weekly lesson plan cover sheet or at-a-glance, which maps out your observations of children and the learning domain (or standards) goals for children for the week, individual strategies for children, and a time for teacher reflection. Your weekly plan provides the detailed information about the intentional experiences planned for children, and how you plan to implement them in the classroom.

Many CIRCLES teachers complete the at-a-glance first during their planning meeting before moving into creating their detailed lesson plans for the week. Other CIRCLES teachers prefer to create the detailed plans first, and then follow-up with creating the at-a-glance. The at-a-glance sheet can often be a good overview to show to parents, visitors, or administration when they visit the classroom.

Completing the Lesson Plan Packet

The CIRCLES® Daily Lesson Plan form is designed to facilitate intentional teaching using active and engaged learning strategies. On a weekly basis, the preschool teacher and co-teacher meet to plan the next week's lessons. This meeting should be scheduled at a time that is convenient for both teachers and is considered essential to the effective delivery of the educational program for children and families.

To begin the planning meeting, teachers review the current week, discussing what went well and what might need adjustment. Observations of student performance and anecdotal notes recorded should also be reviewed and discussed. Teachers may ask the following kinds of questions when beginning:

- What did we notice about children's developing skills?
- What information did parents share about their children this week?
- Is more time needed on the goals and curriculum focus emphasized this week?
- Is it time to move on to new goals or other developmental domains or standards?

Using this information along with assessment data, teachers will decide on an instructional focus for the next week.

After recording the instructional focus on the Lesson Plan, teachers will consider each work area of the classroom. Are there materials that might be modified or added to the work areas to address the instructional focus for the week? When children go to an area for Work Time, we would like them to engage with materials that are related to the instructional focus. When appropriate materials are in place, teachers can join children in the work areas and use their interactions to support children in moving toward their learning goals.

The next section of the Lesson Plan allows teachers to plan for the Morning Routine, including Circle Time, Small Group Time, and Work Time for each day of the week. Teachers specify the Big Idea for each day, the targeted learning domains will be noted, and the books, songs and other activities will be described. After planning the morning routine, teachers design their plans for the afternoon areas of focus.

Using Assessment Data to Guide Lesson Planning

When teachers plan and create lesson plans for children on a weekly basis the process should look like this:

1. Teachers and co-teachers set aside a weekly time to plan together. For many teachers this planning time may happen at the end of a teaching week, and before the next week.
2. Bring the following items to the planning meeting:
    a. The current week's lesson plan
    b. Any anecdotal notes written about children during that week.
    c. Any work samples collected from children that week.
    d. Any screening or assessment data collected that week (this will not occur every week but if you have data, please bring it).
    e. Any information about children shared by parents.
    f. Any information about children shared by other school staff or support teams (early intervention, etc.)
    g. Children's files and/or developmental checklists.
3. Next, reflect on the week and jot notes on the lesson plan form (either the at-a-glance or the full form).
    a. What went well? What didn't?
    b. What do the anecdotal notes and work samples tell you about children?
    c. With what materials, or areas of learning, do children need more time for practice?
    d. What skills do children need to practice, or what skills they have mastered?
    e. What learning domains still need focus?
    f. Using the CIRCLES® Developmental Checklists, record where children are in some areas of focus, to keep a running record of child development. Or, you may want to use these checklists on a quarterly or semester basis.
4. From your reflection and discussion, make decisions about your targeted focuses for next week and record on next week's lesson plan cover sheet/at-a-glance.
    a. What observations will guide the lesson plans this week?
    b. What are your targeted Learning Domains or standards?
    c. What are your Big Ideas for the week?
    d. What books and materials do you need to obtain or add to the environment?
5. Once you have decided on the targeted domains, objectives for children, and materials needed, plan for each day of the week.
    a. What experiences will you provide in the Morning Routine? What targeted skill development can you do in the afternoon?
    b. How will you support children?
    c. What skills will you observe for?
    d. What questions will you ask children?

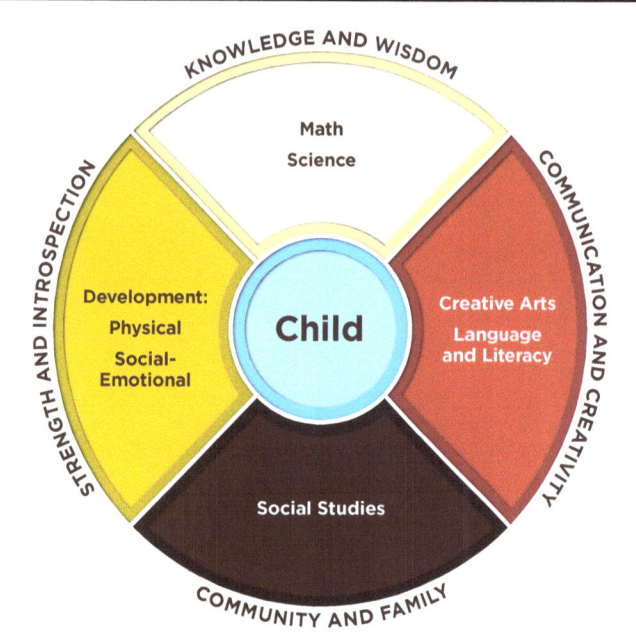

CIRCLES® Early Childhood Learning Domains

Approaches to Learning

Wonder and Curiosity

Initiative and Persistence

Cooperation and Confidence

Reflection

Problem Solving and Experimentation

Engagement and Attentiveness

Developing Habits

Imagination and Creativity

Knowledge And Wisdom

Math Domain

- Counting
- Operations
- Measurement
- Geometry

Science Domain

- Observation and Inquiry
- Investigation
- Make and Express Conclusions
- Interpret and Share Learning

Communications And Creativity

Language and Literacy Domain

- Writing
- Oral Language
- Phonological Awareness
- Alphabet Knowledge and Print Awareness

Creative Arts Domain

- Art
- Music
- Movement
- Dramatic Play

Community And Family

Social Studies Domain

- Self and Others
- Family Relationships
- Classroom Community
- Neighborhood Community

Strength And Introspection

Physical Domain

- Gross Motor
- Fine Motor
- Sensory
- Health and Nutrition
- Safety

Social Emotional Development Domain

- Self-Awareness
- Trust and Respect
- Responsibility for Self

CIRCLES EARLY CHILDHOOD LEARNING DOMAINS, 3-5 YEARS

Children should know and be able to do these skills by kindergarten entry

Approaches To Learning

A preschooler's daily routine and environment is designed to promote various approaches to learning. In the CIRCLES Curriculum, the learning times for children—specifically the Morning Routine—provide multiple opportunities for children to create and approach their own learning in various ways. These **Approaches to Learning** span and support all of the **Domains of Learning** that follow in this document.

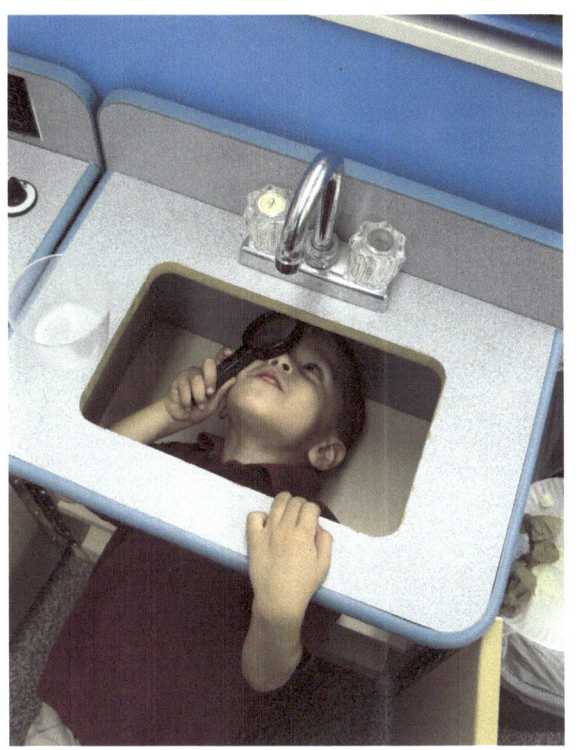

Wonder and Curiosity

- Show interest in new learning experiences
- Ask questions and pose new ideas and situations

Initiative and Persistence

- Initiate learning and explore new ideas
- Show independence in interaction and choices
- Continue, persevere, and finish challenging tasks

Cooperation and Confidence

- Play in groups and work collaboratively and confidently with others
- Show self-assurance in a variety of circumstances

Reflection

- Think about, recall, and review experiences and learning

Problem Solving and Experimentation

- Use trial and error and exploration to complete tasks

Engagement and Attentiveness

- Focus intently on an activity, experience of interest

Develop Habits

- Follow routines daily
- Demonstrate knowledge of a repeated task or routine

Imagination and Creativity

- Show the ability to think and express unique ideas
- Offer unusual ideas to solve a problem or create something new

KNOWLEDGE AND WISDOM

Math Domain

Preschool children construct their knowledge of math through their prior knowledge and experiences, their interactions with the world around them, their experiences with real objects, and through events in their daily lives. Their sense of curiosity and exploration fuels their need to know more. Preschool teachers support math experiences by adding materials to the children's environment so that children can incorporate math into their work and play. Lesson plans provide many active learning experiences which can include math concepts.

Counting

Children will:

- Understand and use numbers daily
- Count up to 10 items
- Identify numbers in the environment
- Write numbers from 1-10
- Count objects in sequence and share "how many"
- Count objects using one-to-one correspondence
- Count number of items in a group
- Match numbers from 1-10 with the quantities they represent
- Identify "less than," "equal to," or "more than" with group of objects

Operations

Children will:

- Match, sort, and group (classify) items according to one or two attributes
- Describe changes in number of sets of objects when combined or separated
- Understand that adding to (or taking away) objects changes the group
- Understand that putting two groups of objects together makes a bigger group
- Understand that splitting a group apart will make more than one group
- Compare and contrast objects, events, and experiences
- Arrange items into a pattern and describe (red, blue, red, blue; big, bigger, biggest)
- Recognize and duplicate patterns
- Understand the sequence and concepts of time (what comes next; yesterday/tomorrow)

Measurement

Children will:

- Use non-standard measures (hands, boxes, rope) to measure objects
- Use standard measures (ruler, measuring cup, scales) for simple measuring tasks
- Participate in measuring activities
- Uses descriptive words for size, amount, and comparisons (more, less, same as, fewer, greater than)
- Compare objects and understands terms (bigger, longer, faster, taller)

Geometry

Children will:

- Name basic shapes
- Identify basic shapes in the environment
- Compare and describe attributes of shapes
- Put together and take apart shapes (sometimes to make new shapes)
- Understand positional terms (between, inside, under, behind, over, in front, behind, etc.)

KNOWLEDGE AND WISDOM

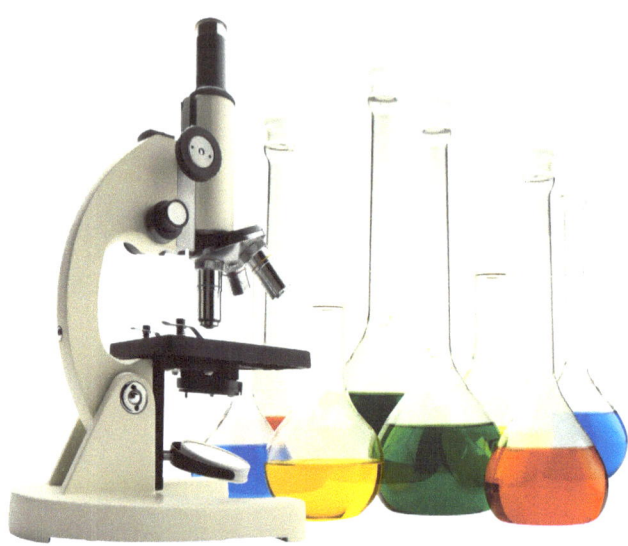

Science Domain

Young children are naturally inquisitive. That curiosity lends itself to observation, asking questions, exploring, manipulating items, and thinking about how things work. They observe, inquire, wonder, investigate, and interpret. All of this is science. Preschool teachers set the stage for science exploration by providing materials and a learning environment where children can feel free to explore, experiment, and be inquisitive—an environment where it is okay to take things apart and put them back together again in a different way. Provide items like magnifying glasses, scales, measuring tools, and water and sand tables in the environment. Incorporate science into small group time and other times of the day.

Observation and Inquiry

Children will:

- Demonstrate curiosity about objects, living things, and natural environments
- Use senses to observe and explore objects, living things, and natural environments
- Examine attributes of objects, living things, and natural environments
- Describe changes in objects, living things, and natural environments
- Observe and describe the relationships between objects, living things, and natural events
- Respond to questions about relationships of objects, living things, and events in the natural environment
- Asks questions about relationships of objects, living things, and natural events in the environment

Investigation

Children will:

- Predict the outcome of investigation based on observation
- Uses a variety of tools and materials to complete a planned task or investigation
- Test predictions through active experimentation
- Change plan if results are different than expected
- Persist with an investigation despite distraction and interruption

Make and Express Conclusions

Children will:

- Compare and contrast the attributes of objects and living things
- Use a variety of materials to record and organize data
- Identify cause and effect relationships
- Form logical conclusions about investigations

Interpret and Share Learning

Children will:

- Share facts about objects, living things, and other natural events in the environment, through words or pictures
- Describe attributes of objects, living things, and natural events. (e.g., weight, texture, flavor, scent, flexibility, and sound)
- Display and interpret data
- Present scientific ideas in a variety of ways

COMMUNICATION AND CREATIVITY

Language and Literacy Domain

Children's early experiences with language and literacy help form the foundation for learning to read. Children's experiences and every day routines provide the necessary learning environment to make language and literacy happen—at home, at school, and in the community. Preschool teachers are respectful and supportive of children's culture and Native language while learning two languages.

The National Early Literacy Panel (NELP, 2008), a group of researchers charged with the task of determining the best predictors for preschool children's success in learning how to read, reviewed the evidence base of research to share the most important concepts to teach. Those concepts include writing, oral language development, phonological awareness, alphabet knowledge, and print awareness. The domains below include these concepts and skills.

Writing

Children will:

- Understand the purpose for writing
- Use scribbles, drawings, letter-like forms, and letters to represent words
- Talk about their writing and "read" it to others
- Experiment with different writing tools and materials
- Identify and write the letters of the alphabet
- Identify and write own first name
- Identify and write many upper and lower case letters
- Understand simple punctuation and capitalization
- Use invented spelling

Oral Language

Children will:

- Listen to conversations, initiate, and engage in conversations with others
- Take turns in conversation with others, using back and forth exchanges
- Listen to, respond to, retell, and ask questions about stories
- Follow simple one- or two-step directions
- Speak clearly in English to be understood by adults and children
- Speak or attempt to speak in Native language (if appropriate)
- Use increasingly complex vocabulary and sentences
- Use language, drawings, and props to pretend, create, and communicate
- Respond to open-ended questions with more than a one-word response

- Repeat new words and phrases learned from story books
- Extend and elaborate on conversations, adding new words and ideas
- Talk about the meanings of words
- Name objects, actions, and attributes with simple words
- Sort objects into categories and name the category

Phonological Awareness

Children will:

- Listen to and participate in saying poems, chants, rhymes, and finger plays
- Recognize that letters have sounds
- Make the sounds of letters (phonemes)
- Participate in sound and word games and orally manipulate sounds (onset-rime, phonemes)
- Identify words with same ending sound (rhyme)
- Identify words with same beginning sound (alliteration)
- Break a word into syllables, such as: basket = /bas/ + /ket/
- Clap words in a sentence or syllables in words
- Identify individual sounds in some simple words, /h/ /a/ /t/

Alphabet Knowledge & Print Awareness

Children will:

- Recognize that letters are symbols that make up words
- Recognize the first letter of own name
- Recognize first name in print
- Match some letter names to printed form
- Identify all letters of the alphabet
- Identify the printed letter, say its name, and make its sound
- Understand environmental print, signs, and symbols
- Understand that print has meaning
- Understand that words said can be written down and read by others
- Use appropriate book handling skills (holds book correctly, turns pages right to left, points to print on page)
- Track/follow words on a page from left to right, top to bottom
- Identify the parts of a book: front and back cover, spine, title, page, author, illustrator
- Participate in group reading activities and show appreciation for books
- Enjoy a variety of children's book genres
- Tell others about the meaning of words and pictures
- Know the difference between pictures/illustrations and letters/words.
- Predict what might happen in a book by looking at the cover or pictures
- Tell what happened in the beginning, middle, and end of a story

COMMUNICATION AND CREATIVITY

Creative Arts Domain

Art nurtures a child's spirit and sparks his imagination. Encourage preschool children to express their ideas, thoughts, emotions, and creativity using art materials, music, movement and dance, and dramatic play. Provide varied and unique materials for children to explore their creativity. Allow them to explore and manipulate. Use both real and found materials in addition to store bought items. Let children get messy and see what they create. Creative arts experiences connect to other learning domains—for example, Science (mixing colors), Physical (movement and dance), Social Studies (dramatic play), Math (counting beats and rhythm), Language and Literacy (singing songs), Social-Emotional (rocking a baby doll, pretending to read to a teddy bear)—so incorporate the arts into your lesson plans throughout the daily routine.

Art

Children will:

- Use a variety of materials, media, tools, and processes to create art
- Participate in creative activities in their home, community, or culture
- Relate pictures and drawings to real places and things
- Express choices when doing art activities
- Change the shape of objects to make something new

Music

Children will:

- Explore and experiment with a variety of musical instruments or sounds
- Listen, participate in, and respond to different types of music
- Create music of own culture
- Talk about, respond to, and describe music created by self and others

Movement

Children will:

- Use creative movement to express ideas, experiences, or feelings
- Show growth in moving in time to different patterns of beat and rhythm
- Participate in dance and movement activities at school, home, and in the community

Dramatic Play

Children will:

- Participate in dramatic play activities that become more complex
- Show growing creativity and imagination in using materials and while assuming different roles in dramatic play
- Participate in dramatic play that reflects the routines, rituals, and celebrations of the home, school, community, and culture
- Adds details and new elements to dramatic play over time

COMMUNITY AND FAMILY

Social Studies Domain

Social studies begin with children understanding relationships—their relationship in the family, the classroom, and their community. By learning to share materials, work collaboratively, and understand how their actions affect others, children learn how to survive in a larger world. Dramatic play activities mimic a social world for children—this is why you see children imitating the "real world" in the House and Block areas. Provide materials for children to role-play and provide them with the tools for getting along as they work together.

Self and Others

Children will:

- Describe characteristics of self
- Compare characteristics of self with others
- Express individuality
- Recognize that places where people live make up a community

Family Relationships

Children will:

- View self as a member of a family, clan, or tribe
- Identify family members (mother, father, sister, aunt)
- Use language to identify family members' roles
- Describe family culture and tradition
- Understand similarities and differences of families

Classroom Community

Children will:

- Understand and follow classroom routines
- Perform jobs and responsibilities
- Work with other children in pairs, triads, and small groups
- Work independently when appropriate
- Problem solve issues working alongside others

Neighborhood Community

Children will:

- Understand how people in a community or tribe help each other
- Show awareness of other cultures
- Show awareness of own culture
- Name community, state, and/or reservation in which he/she lives
- Describe physical characteristics of community in which he/she lives
- Identify community helpers and leaders

STRENGTH AND INTROSPECTION

Physical Development

Children gain coordination, stamina, strength, and flexibility as they grow. Preschool children need opportunities for movement and exercise in both large and small ways. Plan daily experiences for children that allow them to use and control their gross (large muscle) and fine (small muscle) motor movements. Young children can also learn how to be safe and healthy, to begin healthy habits, and recognize unsafe situations. Provide these types of experiences within children's every day routines and experiences.

Gross Motor

Children will:

- Move with balance and control
- Participate in games and outdoor play
- Coordinate movements to perform tasks
- Use and work the large muscles of body (trunk, legs, arms)

Fine Motor

Children will:

- Use fingers and hands to manipulate toys, materials, and devices
- Use eye-hand coordination, strength, and control to perform tasks
- Use pincer grasp to pick up and move small objects
- Work to hold pencil with a tripod grasp

Sensory

Children will:

- Exhibit awareness of the five senses
- Exhibit awareness of own body and how it works
- Exhibit awareness of space and items around self

Health and Nutrition

Children will:

- Perform self-care tasks independently (hygiene, personal needs)
- Show growing independence in making good food choices

Safety

Children will:

- Show knowledge of safety rules and routines
- Listen to and follow adult direction during emergencies
- Know how and when to seek help
- Navigate home, school, and community environments safely

STRENGTH AND INTROSPECTION

Social Emotional Development

Social-Emotional development is the foundation of children's cognitive development and lifelong learning. Social and emotional competence is rooted in the relationships children experience in the early years of their lives. Early relationships help children understand themselves, form positive social relationships, relate to adults and children outside their family, and act responsibly toward themselves and others. When children are socially and emotionally ready for school, the transition from home to school is more likely to be successful.

Self-Awareness

Children will:

- Demonstrate knowledge of personal identity
- Demonstrate self-confidence and awareness of abilities
- Show awareness of similarities and differences between self and others
- Make personal preferences known
- Express and describe feelings
- Express strong feelings in appropriate ways
- Associate emotions with words, facial expressions, and behaviors

Trust and Respect

Children will:

- Respond when others initiate interaction
- Respond to affection
- Initiate and sustain positive interactions with others
- Show care, concern, sympathy, and empathy for others
- Resolve conflict in a positive way

Responsibility for Self

Children will:

- Regulate own behaviors and responses
- Manage transitions, daily routines, and unexpected events
- Understand and follow consistent rules
- Accept the consequences of positive or negative actions
- Take responsibility for personal needs
- Respond to requests from adults
- Ask permission to use items that belong to others
- Defend own rights and those of others
- Use courteous words and actions
- Participate in daily cleanup
- Show respect for toys and materials

RECORDING ANECDOTAL NOTES

Child: Date: Section of Day:	Child: Date: Section of Day:
Child: Date: Section of Day:	Child: Date: Section of Day:
Child: Date: Section of Day:	Child: Date: Section of Day:

RECORDING ANECDOTAL NOTES

Child: Date: Section of Day:	Child: Date: Section of Day:
Child: Date: Section of Day:	Child: Date: Section of Day:
Child: Date: Section of Day:	Child: Date: Section of Day:

CIRCLES LEARNING DOMAINS CHECKLISTS – 3-5 YEARS

Child Name_____ Fall Date/Spring Date _____ / _____ Teacher _____

Approaches To Learning

Children should know and be able to do these skills by kindergarten entry.

	Fall			Spring		
Wonder and Curiosity	Beginning	Emergent	Proficient	Beginning	Emergent	Proficient
Shows interest in new learning experiences						
Asks questions and poses new ideas and situations						
Initiative and Persistence						
Initiates learning and explores new ideas						
Shows independence in interaction and choices						
Continues, perseveres, and finishes challenging tasks						
Cooperation and Confidence						
Plays in groups and can work collaboratively and confidently with others						
Shows self-assurance in a variety of circumstances						
Reflection						
Thinks about, recalls, and reviews experiences and learning						
Problem Solving and Experimentation						
Seeks answers to problems Uses trial and error and exploration to complete tasks						
Engagement and Attentiveness						
Focuses intently on an activity, experience of interest						
Develop Habits						
Follows routines daily						
Imagination and Creativity Shows the ability to think and express unique ideas						
Offers unusual ideas to solve a problem or create something new						

Beginning = The child is beginning to show the ability to do this skill, does it infrequently and inconsistently.

Emergent = The child shows emerging tendencies in her or his ability to do the skill, and completes it correctly more times than incorrectly.

Proficient = The child is proficient or has mastered the skill, and does it correctly with frequency and consistency.

CIRCLES LEARNING DOMAINS CHECKLISTS – 3-5 YEARS

Child Name_____ Fall Date/Spring Date _____ /_____ Teacher _____

Knowledge And Wisdom — Math Domain

Children should know and be able to do these skills by kindergarten entry.

	Fall			Spring		
Counting	Beginning	Emergent	Proficient	Beginning	Emergent	Proficient
Understands and uses numbers daily						
Counts numbers up to 10 items						
Identifies numbers in the environment						
Writes numbers from 1-10						
Counts objects using one-to-one correspondence						
Counts number of items in a group						
Matches numbers from 1-10 with the quantities they represent						
Identifies "less than" "equal to" or "more than" with groups of objects						
Operations						
Matches, sorts, and groups (classifies) items according to one or two attributes						
Describes changes in number of sets of objects when combined or separated						
Understands that adding to (or taking away) objects changes the group						
Understands that putting two groups of objects together makes a bigger group						
Understands that splitting a group apart will make more than one group						
Compares and contrasts objects, events, and experiences						
Arranges items into a pattern and can describe (red, blue, red, blue; big, bigger, biggest)						
Recognizes and duplicates patterns						
Understands the sequence and concepts of time (what comes next; yesterday/tomorrow)						
Measurement						
Uses non-standard measures to measure objects (hands, boxes, rope)						
Participates in measuring activities						
Uses descriptive words for size, amount, and comparisons (more, less, same as, fewer, greater than)						
Compares objects and understands terms (bigger, longer, faster)						
Geometry						
Names basic shapes						
Identifies basic shapes in the environment						
Compares and describes attributes of shapes						
Puts together and takes apart shapes (sometimes to make new shapes)						
Understands positional terms (between, inside, under, behind, over, in front, behind, etc.)						

CIRCLES LEARNING DOMAINS CHECKLISTS – 3-5 YEARS

Child Name_____ Fall Date/Spring Date _____/_____ Teacher _____

Knowledge And Wisdom — Science Domain

Children should know and be able to do these skills by kindergarten entry.

	Fall			Spring		
Observation and Inquiry	Beginning	Emergent	Proficient	Beginning	Emergent	Proficient
Demonstrates curiosity about objects, living things, and natural environments						
Use senses to observe and explore objects, living things, and natural environments						
Examines attributes of objects, living things, and natural environments						
Describes changes in objects, living things, and natural environments						
Observes and describes the relationships between objects, living things and natural events						
Responds to questions about relationships of objects, living things, and events in the natural environment						
Asks questions about relationships of objects, living things, and natural events in the environment						
Investigation						
Predicts the outcome of investigation based on observation						
Uses a variety of tools and materials to complete a planned task or investigation						
Tests predictions through active experimentation						
Changes plan if results are different than expected						
Persists with an investigation despite distraction and interruption						
Make and Express Conclusions						
Compares and contrast the attributes of objects and living things						
Uses a variety of materials to record and organize data						
Identifies cause and effect relationships						
Forms logical conclusions about investigations						
Interpret and Share Learning						
Shares facts about objects, living things, and other natural events in the environment through words or pictures						
Describes attributes of objects, living things, and natural events. (e.g. weight, texture, flavor, scent, flexibility, and sound)						
Displays and interpret data						
Presents scientific ideas in a variety of ways						

CIRCLES LEARNING DOMAINS CHECKLISTS – 3-5 YEARS

Child Name_____ Fall Date/Spring Date _____ /_____ Teacher _____

Communication And Creativity — Language and Literacy Domain

Children should know and be able to do these skills by kindergarten entry.

	Fall			Spring		
Writing	Beginning	Emergent	Proficient	Beginning	Emergent	Proficient
Understands the purpose for writing						
Uses scribbles, drawings, letter-like forms, and letters to represent words or stories						
Talks about own writing and "reads" it to others						
Experiments with different writing tools and materials						
Identifies and writes the letters of the alphabet						
Identifies and writes own first name						
Identifies and writes many upper and lower case letters						
Understands simple punctuation and capitalization						
Uses invented spelling						
Oral Language						
Listens to, initiates, and engages in conversations with others						
Takes turns in conversation with others, using back and forth exchanges						
Listens to, responds, retells, and asks questions about stories						
Follows simple one- or two-step directions						
Speaks clearly in English to be understood by adults and children						
Speaks or attempts to speak in Native language (if appropriate)						
Uses increasingly complex vocabulary and sentences						
Uses language, drawings, and props to pretend, create, and communicate						
Responds to open-ended questions with more than a one-word response						
Repeats new words and phrases learned from story books						
Extends and elaborates on conversations, adding new words and ideas						
Talks about the meanings of words						
Names objects, actions, and attributes with simple words						
Sorts objects into categories and names the category						
Phonological Awareness						
Listens to and participates in saying poems, chants, rhymes, and finger plays						

(Communication And Creativity Language and Literacy Domain Continued)

	Fall			Spring		
	Beginning	Emergent	Proficient	Beginning	Emergent	Proficient
Recognizes that letters have sounds						
Makes the sounds of letters (phonemes)						
Participates in sound and word games and orally manipulates sounds (onset-rime, phonemes)						
Identifies words with same ending sound (rhyme)						
Breaks a word into syllables, such as: basket = /bas/ + /ket/						
Claps words in a sentence or syllables in words						
Identifies individual sounds in some simple words, /h/ /a/ /t/						
Alphabet Knowledge & Print Awareness						
Recognizes that letters are symbols that make up words						
Recognizes the first letter of own name						
Recognizes first name in print						
Matches some letter names to printed form						
Identifies all letters of the alphabet						
Identifies the printed letter, say its name, and make its sound						
Understands environmental print, signs, and symbols						
Understands that print has meaning						
Understands that words said can be written down and read by others						
Uses appropriate book handling skills (holds book correctly, turns pages right to left, points to print on page)						
Tracks/follows words on a page from left to right, top to bottom						
Identifies the parts of a book: front and back cover, spine, title page, author, illustrator						
Participates in group reading activities and shows appreciation for books and reading						
Enjoys a variety of children's book genres						
Tells others about the meaning of words and pictures						
Knows the difference between pictures/illustrations and letters/words.						
Predicts what might happen in a book by looking at the cover or pictures						
Tells what happened in the beginning, middle, and end of a story						

CIRCLES LEARNING DOMAINS CHECKLISTS – 3-5 YEARS

Child Name_____ Fall Date/Spring Date _____ /_____ Teacher _____

Communication And Creativity — Creative Arts Domain

Children should know and be able to do these skills by kindergarten entry.

	Fall			Spring		
Art	Beginning	Emergent	Proficient	Beginning	Emergent	Proficient
Uses a variety of materials, media, tools, and processes to create art						
Participates in creative activities in child's home, school, community/tribe						
Relates pictures and drawings to real places and things						
Expresses choices when doing art activities						
Changes the shape of objects to make something new						
Music						
Explores and experiments with a variety of musical instruments or sounds						
Listens, participates in, and responds to different types of music						
Creates music of own culture						
Talks about, responds to, and describes music created by self and others						
Movement						
Uses creative movement to express ideas, experiences, or feelings						
Shows growth in moving in time to different patterns of beat and rhythm						
Participates in dance and movement activities at school, home, and in the community						
Dramatic Play						
Participates in dramatic play activities that become more complex						
Shows growing creativity and imagination in using materials and while assuming different roles in dramatic play						
Participates in dramatic play that reflects the routines, rituals, and celebrations of the home, school, community, and culture						
Adds details and new elements to dramatic play over time						

CIRCLES LEARNING DOMAINS CHECKLISTS – 3-5 YEARS

Child Name_____ Fall Date/Spring Date _____ / _____ Teacher _____

Community And Family — Social Studies Domain

Children should know and be able to do these skills by kindergarten entry.

	Fall			Spring		
Self and Others	Beginning	Emergent	Proficient	Beginning	Emergent	Proficient
Describes characteristics of self						
Compares characteristics of self with others						
Expresses individuality						
Recognizes that places where people live make up a community						
Family Relationships						
Views self as a member of a family, clan, or tribe						
Identifies family members (mother, father, sister, aunt)						
Uses language to identify family member roles						
Describes family culture and tradition						
Understands similarities and differences of families						
Classroom Community						
Understands and follows classroom routines						
Performs jobs and responsibilities						
Works with other children in pairs, triads, and small groups						
Works independently when appropriate						
Problem solves issues working alongside others						
Neighborhood Community						
Understands how people in a community or tribe help each other						
Shows awareness of other cultures						
Shows awareness of own culture						
Names community, state, and/or reservation in which he/she lives						
Describes physical characteristics of community in which he/she lives						
Identifies community helpers and leaders						

CIRCLES LEARNING DOMAINS CHECKLISTS – 3-5 YEARS

Child Name_____ Fall Date/Spring Date _____ /_____ Teacher _____

Strength And Introspection — Physical Development

Children should know and be able to do these skills by kindergarten entry.

	Fall			Spring		
Gross Motor	Beginning	Emergent	Proficient	Beginning	Emergent	Proficient
Moves with balance and control						
Participates in games and outdoor play						
Coordinates movements to perform tasks						
Uses and works the large muscles of body (trunk, legs, arms)						
Fine Motor						
Uses fingers and hands to manipulate toys, materials, and devices						
Uses eye-hand coordination, strength, and control to perform tasks						
Uses pincer grasp to pick up and move small objects						
Works to hold pencil with a tripod grasp						
Sensory						
Exhibits awareness of the five senses						
Exhibits awareness of own body and how it works						
Exhibits awareness of space and items around self						
Health and Nutrition						
Performs self-care tasks independently (hygiene, personal needs)						
Shows growing independence in making good food choices						
Safety						
Shows knowledge of safety rules and routines						
Listens to and follows adult direction during emergencies						
Knows how and when to seek help						
Navigates home, school, and community environments safely						

CIRCLES LEARNING DOMAINS CHECKLISTS – 3-5 YEARS

Child Name_____ Fall Date/Spring Date _____ /_____ Teacher _____

Social Emotional Development

Children should know and be able to do these skills by kindergarten entry.

	Fall			Spring		
Self Awareness	Beginning	Emergent	Proficient	Beginning	Emergent	Proficient
Demonstrates knowledge of personal identity						
Demonstrates self-confidence and awareness of abilities						
Shows awareness of similarities and differences between self and others						
Makes personal preferences known						
Expresses and describe feelings						
Expresses strong feelings in appropriate ways						
Associates emotions with words, facial expressions, and behaviors						
Trust and Respect						
Responds when others initiate interaction						
Responds to affection						
Initiates and sustains positive interactions with others						
Shows care, concern, sympathy, and empathy for others						
Resolves conflict in a positive way						
Responsibility for Self						
Regulates own behaviors and responses						
Manages transitions, daily routines, and unexpected events						
Understands and follows consistent rules						
Accepts the consequences of positive or negative actions						
Takes responsibility for personal needs						
Responds to requests from adults						
Asks permission to use items that belong to others						
Defends own rights and those of others						
Uses courteous words and actions						
Participates in daily cleanup						
Shows respect for toys and materials						

CIRCLES DAILY/WEEKLY LESSON PLAN

Week (date)					
The Big Idea					
	Day 1	Day 2	Day 3	Day 4	
The Big Idea for today: (CT, SGT, WT)					
Observations that led to this idea (why this big idea?)					
Learning Domain *Connections:* *Area:* *Domain:* *Children will:*					
Approaches to Learning:					
Circle Time					
Welcome and Community Building **How I will introduce The Big Idea**					
What else I will do today in CT:					
Books or materials I need:					
Related Domains of Learning:					
Small Group Time					
Books or materials I will need:					
Teacher: Demonstrate the Big Idea *What I will do:*					
Children: Watch/Listen then Do *Teacher Observes/Supports* **Reminder—jot down anecdotal notes* *What I will observe for: What questions might I ask?*					
Clean-up **Transition to Work Time** *What I will do/say:*					

Work Time (Wonder-Work-Share)				
Books or materials to add to the environment:				
How I will help children Plan/Wonder				
What I will observe for during Work Time: *Reminder—jot down anecdotal notes*				
Review/Reflect (Share) Closing Circle (5-10 minutes) *How I will help children review and reflect on their morning work:*				
Afternoon Schedule • **Snack/Lunch** (teach handwashing, serving, lining up procedures) • **PACT Time** (with parent-child reading time) • **Rest Time** (with read alouds) • **Specials** (P.E., Art, Computer, Culture, Library) • **Extended/Focused Small Group Times** • **Additional Work Time** **Closing Circle Time** (Read a Native book of choice)				
Daily Reflection				

CIRCLES WEEKLY LESSON PLAN AT-A-GLANCE

Dates	Circles Weekly Planning Cover Sheet – At-A-Glance
Previous Week's Observations	
Targeted Learning Domains	
The Big Idea	Day 1 Day 2 Day 3 Day 4 Day 5
Related Learning Domains	
Books or Materials to add to the Learning Environment	

CIRCLES® DAILY LESSON PLAN (SAMPLE/DETAILED)

Week (date)	Day 1 – First Day of School

The Big Idea

Observations that led to this idea:

- Review any information you have on the children such as folders from transitioning programs, last year's data of returning children, and information shared by parents

Learning Domain Connections:

Area: Strength and Introspection; *Domain:* Social Emotional Development: Responsibility for Self
Children will:

- Regulate behaviors and responses
- Manage transitions and daily routine

Approaches to Learning: Developing Habits: Following routines

The Big Idea for today: Learning the daily routine

Circle Time (5-15 minutes)

Welcome and Community Building

How I will introduce The Big Idea

Today boys and girls we are going to learn about our preschool day.

What I will do today:

- Greet each child and invite into the circle
- Share a welcome song with names of each child. Invite children's participation
- Talk about Circle Time—the part of the day right now. Read the pages on Circle Time from the book, *It's Time for Preschool* by Esme Raji Codell. Show the pictures and talk about what is happening.
- Establish a few classroom guidelines, such as listening while in Circle Time, hands in lap, watching the teacher, where the restroom is, and how to get water.
- Talk about Circle Time being one part the daily routine. Show the Daily Routine schedule posted on the wall and talk about how it works.
- Read the book: *The Night Before Preschool* by Natasha Wing. Question: Did you feel like the boy in the story last night? Talk about their responses and how even though we sometimes worry, preschool is fun.
- Close with a Native song, book, story, or words to learn

Books or materials I need:

- *It's Time for Preschool* and *The Night Before Preschool*
- The posted Daily Routine

Related Domains of Learning:

Language and Literacy: Identifying name, participate in reading activities

Social Emotional: Understand and follow consistent rules

Small Group Time (10-20 minutes)

Books or materials I will need:

- Sets of cards that represent the morning routine (and look like what is posted on the wall, but smaller)

Teacher: Demonstrate/Model The Big Idea

What I will do:

- Show children the DR (daily routine) cards. Talk about putting them in order. Place the cards on the table and use words like first, second, next, etc.
- Provide small groups of children with the DR cards. Children can work cooperatively or alone

Children: Watch/Listen then Do

Teacher Observes/Supports *Reminder—jot down anecdotal notes*

What I will observe for:

- How children approach putting the cards in order
- How they work together to solve a problem

What questions might I ask?

- Where in the classroom could we look to help us find the right sequence?

Clean up

Related Domains of Learning:

Math: Understand sequence and concepts of time in daily routines

Social Studies: Work with other children

Work Time (Wonder-Work-Share) (1 hour)

Books or materials to add to the environment:

- Open the House and Block Areas today with basic materials. Add more materials as the weeks progress.

Transition to Work Time (5-10 minutes)

What I will do/say:

- Tell children about Work Time and choosing a place to work. Read the pages on Time to Play in the book *It's Time for Preschool*. Look at the pages and talk about what children are doing.
- Take a walk with children around the room and talk about the two learning areas open today—House Area and Block Area. Come back to the SGT tables

How I will help children plan/Wonder (5 minutes)

- Show children cards with pictures of the two learning areas (House and Block). Ask children to find the same card (label) in the classroom, matching the card to the learning area. Have children say the name of the area.
- Help children choose an area to work in today and support as they choose materials to work with

What I will observe for during Work Time: (40-45 minutes) *Reminder—jot down anecdotal notes*

- How children approach the areas. Which areas they choose
- How they play with others
- Which children need support
- Help to manage cleanup and moving to new areas

Review/Reflect (Share) Closing Circle (5-10 minutes)

How I will help children review and reflect on their morning work:

- Bring children back into large group Circle Time
- Using the Learning Area cards to review and reflect where children played. Hold up a card. "Who played in this area?" "What is this area called?" "What did you do there?"
- Look again at the pages in play in *It's Time for Preschool*. Did anyone do any work like the children in the picture? Ask a few more open-ended questions

Related Domains of Learning:

Social Emotional Development: Ask permission to use items others are using. Participate in daily **cleanup.**

Daily Reflection

Week (date)	Day 2

The Big Idea

Observations that led to this idea:

- Older children guiding young children; children still unsure of routine; children unsure of how to use materials in learning area; cleaning up

Learning Domain Connections:

Area: Strength and Introspection; Domain: Social Emotional Development: Responsibility for Self

Children will:

- Regulate behaviors and responses
- Manage transitions and daily routines
- Participate in clean up; show respect for toys and materials

Approaches to Learning: Developing Habits; Wonder and Curiosity: Interest in new learning experiences

The Big Idea for today: Learning the daily routine

Circle Time (5-15 minutes)

Welcome and Community Building

How I will introduce The Big Idea

Today we will practice the daily routine.

What I will do today:

- Greet each child and invite into the circle
- Remind children of simple guidelines discussed yesterday
- Share the same welcome song with names of the children; invite their participation
- Read the book: *Maisy Goes to Preschool* by Lucy Cousins. Talk about Maisy's day. "How does Maisy's day look like our day?" Ask and open-ended question about the book and allow conversation about the story.
- Ask who can show us on the Daily Routine chart where we are right now in the day.
- Close with a Native song, book, story, or words to learn

Books or materials I need:

- *Maisy Goes to Preschool*

Related Domains of Learning:

Language and Literacy: Identifying name, participate in reading activities

Social Emotional: Understand and follow consistent rules

Small Group Time (10-20 minutes)

Books or materials I will need:

- Choose a few materials from the House Area and the Block Area. For example: Tea set, dishes, baby dolls, clothes, blocks, road signs, animals
- Make sure the shelves are labeled with pictures of each item

Teacher: Demonstrate/Model The Big Idea

What I will do:

- Show children the materials and asked if anyone played with them yesterday
- Using the Learning Area cards from yesterday, match a toy with a Learning Area picture.
- Ask children to pick a toy—would it go in the House or Block Area? Talk about the differences in each.
- Children may sort toys into two piles—Block and House
- Talk about cleaning up and putting toys away when finished. Have the children pick one toy to a Learning Center and match the toy with its picture label on the shelf.

Children: Watch/Listen then Do

Teacher Observes/Supports *Reminder—jot down anecdotal notes*

What I will observe for:

- How children go about choosing where to place the toys.

What questions might I ask?

- Are there other toys like that one in this area?

Clean up

Related Domains of Learning:

Math: Match items with one attribute

Work Time (Wonder-Work-Share) (1-hour)

Books or materials to add to the environment:

- House and Block Areas are open. Make sure all materials from Small Group are placed back in the areas.

Transition to Work Time

What I will do/say:

- Have children sit back at Small Group tables
- Remind children about Work Time and choosing a place to work. Perhaps review the pages from It's Time for Preschool on Time to Play.

How I will help children Plan/Wonder

- Show children cards with pictures of the two learning areas (House and Block). Ask children to find the same card (label) in the classroom, matching the card to the learning area. Have children say the name of the area.
- Help children to the areas and support as they choose materials

What I will observe for during Work Time: *Reminder—jot down anecdotal notes*

- How children approach the areas
- Which areas they choose
- How they play with others
- Which children need support
- Help to manage cleanup and moving to new areas

Review/Reflect (Share) Closing Circle (5-10 minutes)

How I will help children review and reflect on their morning work:

- Bring children back into large group Circle Time
- Using the Learning Area cards to review and reflect where children played. Hold up a card. "Who played in this area?" "What is this area called?" "What did you do there?"
- Re-read Maisy Goes to Preschool. Ask a few open-ended questions. "Was your day today like Maisy's?"

Related Domains of Learning:
Social Emotional Development: Ask permission to use items others are using. Participate in daily cleanup.

Daily Reflection

Week (date)	Day 3

The Big Idea

Observations that led to this idea: Children still unsure of routine; children having difficulty cleaning up before moving to a new area; children not using words to express themselves, especially when sharing toys and materials.

Learning Domain Connections:

Area: Strength and Introspection; *Domain:* Social Emotional Development: Responsibility for Self

Children will:

- Regulate behaviors and responses
- Manage transitions and daily routines
- Participate in clean up; show respect for toys and materials
- Use courteous words and actions

Approaches to Learning: Cooperation; work collaboratively with others. Develop Habits; demonstrate a repeated task.

The Big Idea for today: Taking care of and sharing our materials

Circle Time (5-15 minutes)

Welcome and Community Building

How I will introduce The Big Idea

Today we are going to share and take care of our toys and materials.

What I will do today:

- Greet each child and invite into the circle
- Remind children of simple guidelines discussed yesterday
- Share the same welcome song with names of the children; invite their participation. Take attendance on a white board or chart paper, writing or pointing out each child's name.
- Read the Sharing Time and Manners pages of the book, *It's Time for Preschool*. Show children the pages and ask questions about what children are doing. Talk about sharing and how it's important to share in preschool
- Ask who can show us on the Daily Routine chart where we are right now in the day.
- Close with a Native song, book, story, or words to learn. Tell children we are moving to SGT. Ask a child to point to the SGT block on the DR wall.

Books or materials I need:

- Book: *It's Time for Preschool*
- Chart paper or white board with children's names; markers

Related Domains of Learning:

Language and Literacy: Identifying name, participating in reading activities

Social Studies: Problem solve issues working with others

Small Group Time (10-20 minutes)

Books or materials I will need:

- Materials from the Art Area, such as paper, paint, glue, scissors, found materials, markers, crayons, etc. Have a group of materials for each child, on a tray or in a paper bag. Each child should have their own set.

Teacher: Demonstrate/Model The Big Idea

What I will do:

- Read the Time to Make Stuff pages in It's Time for Preschool and talk with children that sometimes in preschool we use many materials.
- Using your set of materials, show children what you have and how to use it. "I am using these scissors to cut the paper." Demonstrate cutting. "I am using the marker to draw a picture." And so on. Make the demonstration brief.

Children: Watch/Listen then Do

- Next, have children explore their materials and create art. Problem-solve any sharing issues.

Teacher Observes/Supports *Reminder—jot down anecdotal notes*

What I will observe for:

- How children use, and appear interested in, the materials. Which materials do they use most?
- Which children can use the scissors well. Which children are having difficulty?
- Whether children work alone or cooperatively. Are there sharing issues with materials.
- Watch how children clean up and put their materials on their tray or in their bag.

What questions might I ask?

- Do you need other materials? Tell me what you are making?

Clean up: Teach a *Clean-up Song* to children today. Sing this song every time you clean up and put materials away.

Related Domains of Learning:

Art: Use a variety of materials, media, tools, and processes to create art.

Work Time (Wonder-Work-Share) (1 hour)

Books or materials to add to the environment:

- Open the Art Area today, along with House and Block Areas. Provide basic art materials including scissors, paper, glue, found materials, and marking/writing tools.
- Art Area card (labels)

Transition to Work Time

What I will do/say:

- After Small Group cleanup, tell children they will have more time to work on Art projects, if they choose.
- Tell children we are now moving into Work Time. Ask a child to point out WT on the DR chart.

How I will help children Plan/Wonder

- Show children the new Art Area card (label) and match it with the label in the Art Area. Tell children the materials they worked with in SGT belong to the Art Area.
- Ask children to choose an area for Work today by picking a card and saying, "I want to work in the ____ area."
- If a child chooses the Art Area, they can take their tray/bag of materials to the Art Area to work.

What I will observe for during Work Time: *Reminder—jot down anecdotal notes*

- Which learning area children choose for Work Time. Do they always choose the same area?
- How many children chose the new Art Area?
- How are children managing clean-up? How well do they manage sharing and putting away materials?

Review/Reflect (Share) Closing Circle (5-10 minutes)

How I will help children review and reflect on their morning work:

- Sing the Clean-up Song again. Ask children to put the Art materials they used in SGT away in the labeled places. During clean-up, talk to children about what they did in Work Time today.
- Bring children back into large group Circle Time
- Using the Learning Area cards to review and reflect where children played. Hold up a card. "Who played in this area?" "What is this area called?" "What did you do there?"
- Read the first part of *Maisy Goes to Preschool* again from yesterday. Ask a few open-ended questions. "Did Maisy do art? Tell me what she did?" Have a picture-walk discussion of Maisy's paintings.

Related Domains of Learning:

Art: Express choices when creating art activities.

Daily Reflection

Week (date)	Day 4

The Big Idea

Observations that led to this idea: How the children approached the new learning area, Art, and used the materials; any issues with sharing and taking care of materials; children's eagerness to explore new areas and materials; how children are adapting to being in preschool daily.

Learning Domain Connections:

Area: Strength and Introspection; *Domain:* Social Emotional Development: Self Awareness:

Children will:
- Regulate behaviors and responses
- Manage transitions and daily routines
- Participate in clean up; show respect for toys and materials
- Use courteous words and actions
- Express and describe feelings

Approaches to Learning: Confidence; shows self-assurance in a variety of circumstances

The Big Idea for today: Talking about and expressing feelings

Circle Time (10-20 minutes)

Welcome and Community Building

How I will introduce The Big Idea

Today we are going to talk about how we feel about preschool!

What I will do today:
- Greet each child and invite into the circle. Remind children of Circle Time "guidelines." Ask children what part of the day they are in right now. Circle Time!
- Sing the welcome with children and invite their participation.
- Give each child a model of the first letter of his/her name. Take attendance on a white board or chart paper, writing or pointing out each child's name, and the first letter. "Let's see, John is here. John starts with the letter J. John, hold up your letter J. I am putting a check beside your name."
- Read the book, *Llama Mama, Misses Mama* by Anna Dewdney. Talk about how Llama feels in the story at preschool. Ask a few open-ended question and talk about the pictures. "Why does Llama feel alone? Why did Llama miss Mama? How did the other children help Llama feel better?" Ask children if they have ever felt like Llama, and say it is okay to talk about how it feels to miss someone.
- Close with a Native song, book, story, or words to learn. Tell children they are moving to SGT. Ask a child to point to the SGT block on the DR chart.

Books or materials I need:
- Book: *Llama Mama, Misses Mama*
- A letter model for each child—the first letter of their names. This could be a paper letter, plastic or felt letter, a block, etc. Any letter model will do. Upper case preferred.
- Chart paper or white board and markers

Related Domains of Learning:

Language and Literacy: Identifying name, identifying first letter of name; participating in reading activities

Small Group Time (10-20 minutes)

Books or materials I will need:

- Books from the Book Area, enough for one for each child, and to provide choice.
- Book Area card (label)

Teacher: Demonstrate/Model The Big Idea

What I will do:

- Talk about books and stories. Using the *Llama Llama Misses Mama* book, point out the different parts of the book—the front cover, back cover, the words on the cover, and the words inside the book. Open the book to where Mama comes back and talk about the pictures. Ask children what they think is happening on those pages.
- Tell children that there are many books in the classroom for them to read and look at.
- Show the books from the Book Area on the table. Ask each child to pick a book. Again, talk about and point to the front of the book, back of the book, words on a page, and pictures/illustrations.

Children: Watch/Listen then Do

- Let children explore their books, turn the pages, and look at the pictures. Respond to their questions about the books.

Teacher Observes/Supports *Reminder—jot down anecdotal notes*

What I will observe for:

- How children handle the books. Do they hold the book correctly and turn the pages from right to left?
- Do children look at the pictures and talk about what they see?
- Do children have difficulty turning the pages?

What questions might I ask?

- Tell me what is happening in that picture. Why do you think he did that? I wonder what will happen next?

Clean up

- Tell children that books belong in a special place in the classroom called the Book Area. Take them to the book area, tell them it is a new area for Work Time, and show them where to put the books on the bookshelves. Ask children to sit in a circle on the floor in the Book Area.

Related Domains of Learning:

Language and Literacy: Use appropriate book handling skills; identify parts of a book.

Work Time (Wonder-Work-Share) (1 hour)

Books or materials to add to the environment:

- Open the Book Area for children to use during Work Time. Be sure there are enough books for children to choose, plus some additional book related props (puppets, listening devices, alphabet letters, comfortable chairs for reading, etc.)

Transition to Work Time

What I will do/say:

- Tell children we are now moving into Work Time. Ask a child to point out WT on the DR chart.

How I will help children Plan/Wonder

- Show children the new Book Area card (label) and match it with the label in the Book Area. We now have 4 Learning Area cards: House, Block, Art, and Book. Lay the cards out on the floor. Tell children the materials they worked with in SGT belong to the Art Area.
- Ask children to choose an area for Work today by picking a card and saying, "I want to work in the ____ area."
- Support children as they go off to their learning areas and work.

What I will observe for during Work Time: *Reminder—jot down anecdotal notes*

- Which learning area children chose for Work Time. Do they always choose the same area?
- How many children chose the new Book Area?
- How are children managing clean-up? How well do they manage sharing and putting away materials?

Review/Reflect (Share) Closing Circle (5-10 minutes)

How I will help children review and reflect on their morning work:

- Sing the Clean-up Song again. During clean-up, talk to children about what they did in Work Time today.
- Bring children back into large group Circle Time
- Using the Learning Area cards to review and reflect where children played. Hold up a card. "Who played in this area?" "What is this area called?" "What did you do there?"
- Read some more of *Llama Mama, Misses Mama*. Talk about the parts of the book discussed earlier, and ask a few open-ended questions. Point to the words in the book as you read.

Related Domains of Learning:

Language and Literacy: Responding to open-ended questions; know the difference between pictures and words.

Daily Reflection

CIRCLES® Curriculum Application

The Frameworks section of this curriculum provided the foundational information needed to implement a high-quality preschool program. This background information sets the stage and lays the groundwork for program implementation. The Elements section provided specific guidance, strategies, and best practice in seven specific areas of teaching in a preschool classroom.

This Application section divides your school year into four quarters. These quarters are delineated generally, so they do not automatically align with school grading quarters or their equivalents. These four quarters simply divide your school year into fourths, no matter how your school year or program is designed. Whether you are a full year, full day program, or a half-day, nine-month program, this information can easily apply. (We did provide examples of months, but please remember those are only examples and will not apply to all programs.)

As expected, these quarters build upon each other. The first quarter provides guidance for the beginning of the school year. The second quarter adds additional information to build on the first, and so on. The final quarter also discusses transition to the next year of school.

Following the quarterly applications, you will also find a set of lesson plans called The First 20 Days. These lesson plans cover roughly the first 20 days of school for a typical program. Lesson plans vary as the children in the classroom do, so feel free to alter these plans to fit your program. They are provided as an example and reflect the ideas provided in the first quarter application.

Early childhood best practice suggests that teachers always keep the needs, interests, and goals of the children in the classroom in mind, so these quarters are flexibly designed and not prescriptive. Teachers use observation, screening, and assessment to know what to teach and when. These quarters do not tell you what to teach, but rather provide guidance for various elements of teaching. What is provided here are ideas and suggestions—we also know you have many more experiences and ideas to add to the concepts represented here.

Each quarter is divided into six areas:

- Environment
- Routines
- Learning Communities
- Assessment
- Lesson Planning
- Parent Engagement

Following this introduction, you will find the CIRCLES® Curriculum Sequence chart, followed by supporting quarterly application narrative.

CIRCLES CURRICULUM APPLICATION SEQUENCE AT-A-GLANCE

Quarter 1 (Aug-Sept-Oct)	Quarter 2 (Oct-Nov-Dec)	Quarter 3 (Jan-Feb-Mar)	Quarter 4 (April-May-June)
Environment • Familiar photos, items from home, cultural recommendations from parents and elders • Limited number of learning areas • Limited quantity of materials • Clear labeling of materials and equipment • Consistent storage methods • Literacy materials throughout the classroom	**Environment** • Continue to add family and cultural items to the classroom • Introduce new learning areas • Introduce new materials • Add to the literacy materials throughout the classroom • Choose materials for the environment that reflect children's learning needs	**Environment** • Reintroduce children to routines and work areas after the extended time away from school • Introduce new work areas or modify existing areas • Rotate materials and books to maintain interest and challenge developing skills • Place literacy materials for reading and writing throughout the classroom in all learning areas	**Environment** • Introduce new work areas or modify existing areas • Rotate materials to maintain interest and challenge developing skills • Literacy materials throughout
Routines • In place on first day • Short, active Circle Times • Use Small Group Time to introduce materials • Extended Work Time to explore room • Creative Outdoor Time sessions	**Routines** • Extend Circle Time with new activities • Design Small Group Times to address specific learning needs • As needed, create two Small Group Times to address developmental need (higher and lower developmental skill levels) • Introduce new Wonder-Work-Share strategies (planning/reflect) • Evaluate and modify routines and procedures	**Routines** • As children can sit and focus longer, extend and expand Circle Time activities according to their developmental needs • Design Small Group Times to address learning needs • Perhaps focus Small Group Times for transitioning kindergarten students more specifically at kindergarten readiness skills. • Create and share new Wonder-Work-Share strategies for planning and reflection • Increase the complexity of Dialogic Reading prompts and planning/sharing strategies	**Routines** • Continue to extend and expand Circle Time activities according to need • Design Small Group Times to address learning needs • Perhaps focus Small Group Times for transitioning kindergarten students more specifically at kindergarten readiness skills. • Create and share new Wonder-Work-Share strategies for planning and reflection • Increase the complexity of Dialogic Reading prompts and planning/sharing strategies • Introduce four-year-olds to kindergarten classes as appropriate

CIRCLES CURRICULUM APPLICATION SEQUENCE AT-A-GLANCE

Quarter 1 (Aug-Sept-Oct)	Quarter 2 (Oct-Nov-Dec)	Quarter 3 (Jan-Feb-Mar)	Quarter 4 (April-May-June)
Learning Communities • Establish predictable routines • Create a sense of belonging • Help children to feel secure • Help children to begin developing habits to support their learning • Establish a few classroom guidelines • Be consistent	**Learning Communities** • Expand routines and rituals • Be intentional and purposeful in building community • Create deeper personal connections with children and families • Continue to create sense of familiarity and security for children • Foster teamwork and collaborative learning • Support parents as they begin their own learning community and networking opportunities	**Learning Communities** • Extend the children's learning community beyond classroom to include families and the community • Continue to personalize habits and routines • Create new traditions out of routines or continue established ones • Foster teamwork and collaborative learning • Support parents as they begin their own learning community and networking opportunities	**Learning Communities** • Extend the children's learning community beyond classroom to include families and the community • Continue to personalize habits and routines • Create new traditions out of routines or continue established ones • Include transitions to kindergarten as a next step in building community for children and parents • Create a transition plan with parents, kindergarten teacher, and other school personnel

CIRCLES CURRICULUM APPLICATION SEQUENCE AT-A-GLANCE

Quarter 1 (Aug-Sept-Oct)	Quarter 2 (Oct-Nov-Dec)	Quarter 3 (Jan-Feb-Mar)	Quarter 4 (April-May-June)
Assessments	**Assessments**	**Assessments**	**Assessments**
• Begin screening children for general health, dental, hearing, and vision • Observe children and record anecdotal notes • Conduct a formal developmental screening	• Continue to observe children and record anecdotal notes • Watch for children's various approaches to learning and their learning styles • Use information from informal and formal screenings, and observations, in referrals for possible interventions or assistance for children with special needs • Consider administering a language screener or assessment to gauge expressive and/or receptive language. • Complete formal developmental checklists by end of quarter	• Continue to observe children and record anecdotal notes • Watch for children's various approaches to learning and their learning styles • Continue to refer children for services as needed • Follow-up on any outstanding referrals • Monitor intervention activities and services for any child with special needs in your classroom	• Continue to observe children and record anecdotal notes • Watch for children's various approaches to learning and their learning styles • Continue to refer children for services as needed • Follow-up on any outstanding referrals • Monitor intervention activities and services for any child with special needs in your classroom • Administer a post-test language screener or assessment to measure gains in expressive and/or receptive language. • Complete formal developmental checklists by end of quarter • Share appropriate assessment information with transitioning kindergarten teacher

CIRCLES® CURRICULUM APPLICATION SEQUENCE AT-A-GLANCE

Quarter 1 (Aug-Sept-Oct)	Quarter 2 (Oct-Nov-Dec)	Quarter 3 (Jan-Feb-Mar)	Quarter 4 (April-May-June)
Lesson Planning • Use a consistent lesson plan • Plan weekly • Focus on routines, procedures, and community building • Introduce learning areas to children • Focus on children's personal and social development • Gradually introduce classroom materials	**Lesson Planning** • Continue to create lesson plans weekly • Plan lessons based on observation and screening/assessment information collected • Take into account your observations for how children approach learning, and/or their learning styles • Choose materials and design activities throughout the day to address areas of the learning domains • Reflect with Co-teacher about the lesson plans daily	**Lesson Planning** • Continue to create lesson plans weekly • Plan lessons based on observation and screening/assessment information collected • Take into account your observations for how children approach learning, and/or their learning styles • Choose materials and design activities throughout the day to address areas of the learning domains • Reflect with Co-teacher about the lesson plans daily	**Lesson Planning** • Continue to create lesson plans weekly • Plan lessons based on observation and screening/assessment information collected • Take into account your observations for how children approach learning, and/or their learning styles • Choose materials and design activities throughout the day to address areas of the learning domains • Reflect with Co-teacher • Continue discussion with kindergarten teacher about child expectations and kindergarten readiness

CIRCLES® CURRICULUM APPLICATION SEQUENCE AT-A-GLANCE

Quarter 1 (Aug-Sept-Oct)	Quarter 2 (Oct-Nov-Dec)	Quarter 3 (Jan-Feb-Mar)	Quarter 4 (April-May-June)
Parent Engagement • Create a welcome environment for parents with an open-door policy • Begin building rapport and relationships • Ask parents for input on child, family, language and culture • Display family/cultural photos • Host a parent event or open house to introduce parents to the CIRCLES Curriculum • Help parents understand PACT Time® and provide ideas for parents to implement at home	**Parent Engagement** • Form parent-teacher partnerships to support child growth and development • Provide routine and consistent Parent Time topics that support learning • Recognize that parents get involved on different levels • Provide opportunities for parents to participate in PACT Time • Plan Transfer Home experiences, family nights, and a parent-teacher conference • Share assessment information with parents	**Parent Engagement** • Continue to build relationships and rapport with parents and families • Increase intensity of parent education workshops and family events • Focus on children's growth, learning, and development • Move the PACT Time learning from the classroom to the home and to the community • Provide specific parent information about kindergarten readiness and transition for parents with transitioning children	**Parent Engagement** • Parents maintain a supportive home learning environment • Parents provide leadership and mentor other parents • Plan a parent-teacher conference to share child's growth, development and successes, as well as next steps and strategies • Create a kindergarten transition plan with parents • Invite kindergarten teacher to share information during Parent Time for transition and kindergarten readiness • Plan summer activities for families with transitioning kindergarten students

CIRCLES® Curriculum Application Sequence

Implementation Guidance

Quarter One

Environment

As young children enter your classroom for the first time at the beginning of the school year, some will be excited to engage in new adventures and others will be unsure and reluctant to participate. The learning environment you establish must address the needs of every child, offering new and interesting experiences while ensuring familiarity, safety and security.

During the first quarter of the school year, you want children to become familiar with the environment and learn to engage with materials and activities appropriately. To achieve these goals, you'll want to consider the following:

- *Create a welcoming environment* by including items that are familiar to children and reflect their families and homes. A bulletin board that displays photographs of parents and children taken during home visits or orientation sessions; a personal cubby for each child labeled with his/her photograph; a blanket from home and favorite stuffed animal to be used for nap time—these will all communicate "you belong here" to your students.
- *Establish a few basic learning areas* by clearly defining and labeling the spaces within the classroom. To start, be sure to include the Block Area, House Area, Book Area, Art Area, and Technology Area. Starting the year with just a few work areas will allow you to teach children about Work Time, making choices, and managing materials without overwhelming them. Other interest areas can be added once the basic routines are in place.
- Within each interest area, limit the quantity of materials at first until children understand their responsibility for accessing materials to work with and cleaning them up when they are finished. For example, perhaps the Block Area will have a set of wooden blocks, farm animals, vehicles and people figures at the beginning of the year. Additional types of blocks and other props can be added gradually after children understand how to return the blocks to the storage shelves and sort the props into bins.
- Be sure materials in each interest area are stored in an organized and clearly labeled way. When all shelves and containers are clearly labeled, children will quickly learn to independently manage classroom materials.
- From the beginning of the year, place relevant books in each interest area and model their use as you interact with children during Work Time. The integrated use of literacy materials is a foundational element of the CIRCLES curriculum. As you read stories to the dolls in the House Area or refer to a book about buildings in the Block Area children are learning about the importance of literacy in our lives.

Routines

The basic daily routine for your classroom should be in place on the first day of school. You want children to learn the routine as soon as possible and to feel secure in its predictability. Have a visual representation posted on the wall and refer to the elements of the routine as the day progresses. Although time allotments may be adjusted at the beginning of the year, the daily activities should all be in place.

As the year begins, your morning **Circle Time** should be fairly short, active, and engaging to respond to young children's limited attention span. The use of big books that everyone can see will engage children in stories during Circle Time. Teachers can use basic interactive reading strategies right away, including reading expressively and asking simple questions to support listening and promote discussion. Finger plays and songs with movements also encourage participation in active ways.

Small Group Time (SGT) in the first quarter can be used to introduce children to the materials that are available throughout the classroom. Plan open-ended SGT activities by bringing materials from one of the interest areas and encouraging children's exploration and experimentation. Facilitate discussion among the children and support problem-solving as challenges arise. For example, bring play dough from the art area and a set of cookie cutters or other tools. Use the materials yourself and model the use of devices that are not familiar to the children. Or bring a supply of building blocks to the table or simple puzzles or watercolor paints. This is a perfect opportunity to be sure children are aware of materials that are available in the classroom and understand their use. At the end of SGT, ask the children to help return the materials to their storage space and remind them that they can explore further during Work Time. Be flexible with the amount of time allocated for Small Group at the beginning of the year and be ready to transition as interest fades.

As children will be naturally interested in exploring their new classroom, **Work Time** may be the largest block of time in the daily routine during the first quarter. Introduce the Wonder-Work-Share process from the start by using simple planning and sharing strategies. A planning board with photographs of each interest area can facilitate children's responses to "I wonder where you will work today…" by reminding them of their choices. During Work Time, both teachers will be actively engaged with children in the interest areas, offering support when needed, facilitating conversation, and teaching about managing and cleaning up toys and materials. After Work Time, teachers can help children share by revisiting the interest area photographs and asking, "Who played here today?" or bringing actual materials used in the work areas to the circle for children to share. Planning and sharing at the beginning of the year will be simple, but it's important to introduce the process from the start.

Procedures and routines. In addition to these major elements of the daily routine, teachers will need to carefully plan and teach the procedures and routines that are necessary for smooth classroom operations. These will include procedures for:

- Arriving and departing
- Lining up
- Moving through the hallways
- Washing hands
- Serving snacks
- Rest time

It is important to take the time to define expectations and teach the necessary skills and routines in these areas to support children's developing independence and to help them see themselves as part of the classroom community.

Learning Communities

Preschool is a social time as much as it is a learning time. In fact, much of the learning that happens in preschool revolves around children being social. When we are social, we talk, work, play, and solve problems together. We learn the routines of how the classroom works, how the day is structured, and how we interact with others and the elements of the day.

In this first quarter of the year, establishing a learning community is as basic as establishing simple routines. Focus on helping children feel a sense of *predictability*, *belonging*, and *security*.

Children thrive when their days are *predictable*. This brand new world of preschool is a challenging experience for young three- and four-year olds. For many, this may be the first time to spend their days, or part of their day, in a group social situation. Establishing expectations for children can be as simple as creating a few regular habits to help ground students in their day. In this first quarter, start with the kinds of practices listed below. You may have more but remember to start with a few and build.

- **Morning Circle Time** is the first real activity children will gather for each day. This brief time together is important to establish a sense of learning together as a group, or a community of learners. Your morning Circle Time happens daily, at the same time every day. In short, it's predictable! Children know this is when their learning day begins. This time together acts as the transition between arrival time, and ready to learn. Predictability within your Circle Time is also important. Remember, Circle Time should be short at first (perhaps 5-10 minutes) due to limited attention spans.

- For this first quarter, choose two-three experiences to repeat every single day, in the same order. For example:
    - *Morning Message.* Greet children daily with a verbal morning message or greeting.
    - *Read a book* and use some basic read aloud strategies.
    - *Sing a short song* or say a rhyme.
    - *Review the Daily Schedule* posted on the wall. Talk about what comes next.
- **Cues and signals** help children remember the sequence and order of the day. In this first quarter, choose basic cues/signals for a few important ideas. Perhaps a hand in the air means everyone stops what they are doing. A familiar song signals clean up time. Dimming the lights means it is time to prepare for rest.
- **A place for everything (and everything in its place)** is a wise, age-old mantra and a good one. Clearly label shelves in the environment with pictures or objects so that children know on which shelf toys belong.
- **Be consistent**. Whatever routines you establish, always do them in the same way, every day, and have the same daily expectations for children. Preschool-age children's brains are hard-wired to learn with repetition. While doing things at the same time, and in the same way every day may seem boring to you, it is a learning experience for children.

Children thrive within a classroom community that provides them with a **sense of belonging**. Create an inclusive, welcoming environment that supports children and their families.

- **Greet children** at the door every day, say their names, and welcome them into the room. At the end of the day, send them off with a warm good-bye until next time.
- **Identify each child's cubby** or chair with his/her picture and name, so that it clearly identifies the child's space. Having a space of your own within the classroom means "I belong here."
- Place **family pictures** in the classroom. Perhaps have a bulletin board for family events, or for children sharing. Frame snapshots of children and their families, and place them in various areas of the classroom.

Feeling secure within a new environment makes learning so much better. Children feel free to explore and experience new things when they feel safe and secure in their environments, and when their ideas are accepted and important.

- Help children to understand the **expectations of arrival and departure times**. Whether they arrive with a parent or ride a school bus, these beginning and end of day transitions, in and out of school, can sometimes be frightening. Assure children that they don't have to navigate these scary times alone.
- **Post the daily routine schedule** on the wall in such a way that children can "read" and understand what comes next. Simple left-to-right blocks of cards with a picture that represents the element of the schedule is all you need for children at the beginning of the year. Later on, you can add more detail, if you feel children need that. Remember, this posted schedule is for children, not adults, so it should be at their eye level. When children get antsy about when Mom or Granny is coming to pick them up, use the schedule as a tool to help them understand. "In three pictures your Mommy will be here."

- Knowing that **snacks and meals** will arrive on time, and at the same time every day, is comforting to children.
- Children feel safe and at ease when their **personal needs are met**. Knowing they can use the restroom at will, or get a drink of water when needed, not only encourages independence, but contributes to their comfort level in the classroom. When children are comfortable, they feel freer to explore and learn.
- When children speak, offer ideas, and share solutions to a problem, **always respectfully listen and respond**.

Assessments

Assessment during the first quarter of the year is focused on observation and screening. Conduct informal and formal screenings to identify any significant intervention needs and to begin to gather baseline information on children's levels of development and learning.

Observation. Be a good observer of children every day. Make time to stop and slow down for parts of the day and watch how children approach learning and tasks. Record anecdotal notes during this time so you have a written record of where children were at the beginning of the year, to compare with notes taken later in the year.

Screening. We suggest that within the first 45 days of enrollment that each child be screened for overall health, development, dental, hearing and vision. Check with local Child Find, Indian Health Care, and other local medical services to provide these screenings for children. The preschool teacher and co-teacher may work with parents to complete a general health screening, such as the Ages and Stages Questionnaire, with parent input. The results of all screenings will be discussed with the parents and if a need for further evaluation or intervention is indicated, follow-up plans will be developed.

Oral language test. Consider administering a standardized assessment, such as the Expressive One Word Picture Vocabulary Test, to measure children's expressive and/or receptive English vocabulary skills. Such instruments ask children to name objects, actions, or concepts pictured in illustrations. If you administer an oral language assessment not long after children enroll for the school year, you may also want to administer it again at the end of the year as a measure of vocabulary growth.

Lesson Planning

The CIRCLES Daily Lesson Plan is used weekly to establish learning goals, choose materials, and develop activities to meet the needs of children in the program. Because the children's assessment data is limited at the beginning of the year, lesson plans will focus on the materials you want to introduce, the routines you want to teach, and the developmental areas you want to observe.

For example, a lesson plan at the beginning of the year might focus on classroom routines. When planning the week's lessons, teachers will identify the interest areas that will be introduced and particular materials in each that might be helpful for demonstrating management and clean up strategies. They might read books about school and classroom procedures during Circle Time and might teach a clean up song the children will hear regularly. Small Group Time could be planned to introduce materials from the classroom and a whole group motor activity might be introduced during Outside Time. Throughout the week, the emphasis will be on introducing and practicing classroom routines. Teachers will also constantly observe how children are doing with their new learning environment, new friends, and new expectations. For ideas on areas to observe and document, teachers will refer to the CIRCLES Learning Domains (CLD) and the CIRCLES Learning Domains Checklists (CLDC).

For example, in the area of Social Emotional Development on the CLD, the following indicators might be observed as children are learning classroom routines:

- Demonstrates self-confidence
- Manages transitions, daily routines, and unexpected events
- Participates in daily cleanup
- Shows respect for toys and materials

As teachers implement activities that introduce classroom routines, they can be making notes on how children perform these areas of development and will be gathering data that can be used during the next quarter to complete the WSS Checklist.

Additional planning sections at the end of the Lesson Plan Form can be used to remind teachers about screening and assessments to be completed and any follow-up or actions that need to be taken for specific children.

Parent Engagement

Teachers set the climate for parent involvement in the classroom very early in the school year. In the first quarter, it is important to establish relationships and create that positive environment for engagement. Parents need to know they are valued members of the classroom community, and that they are equal partners and supporters of their children's' learning success. Teachers can also help parents set the climate for learning at home. Family-friendly school and classroom environments invite parent involvement. Parents' comfort levels at school also determine their levels of involvement.

Teachers encourage a family-friendly climate by using effective communication skills, relationship building, supportive engagement practices, and parent leadership.

Begin by providing some non-threatening activities parents can participate in with their children to help parents get started. This could be as simple as designating a day of the week to eat lunch or breakfast with their children, an observation of PACT Time® in action (for new parents), or an invitation to an after-school event. Know the comfort levels of your parents and plan accordingly.

In this first quarter:

- Assess your classroom environment. Does it say "Welcome" to families?"
- Welcome parents into your classroom as observers.
- Maintain an open-door policy. Parents and families are always welcome.
- Provide one or two adult-sized chairs in the classroom so that parents or grandparents can sit comfortably when visiting.
- Ask parents what would make them feel more comfortable in the classroom.
- Get parents input on cultural activities or experiences they would like to see their children involved in at school.
- Have displays in the classroom that reflect families, their community, and their cultures (photos, cultural events, family get-togethers, community happenings, etc.)
- Communicate with parents in a variety of ways. Consider their home language and literacy levels. Communicate in ways that all parents can understand.
- Begin building rapport early as children transition into preschool.
- Make personal contacts with families, perhaps conduct a home visit before school begins or within the first few weeks of school.
- Personally invite parents to the school/classroom open house or the first family engagement event of the year.
- Ask parents about their expectations for their children's growth and development.
- Acknowledge that parents know their children best, and that they are the first and best teachers of their children.

Quarter Two

Environment

By the second quarter of the school year, children should be more comfortable in the classroom environment and ready to manage new interest areas, new materials and new challenges.

- Continue to emphasize children's ownership of the classroom environment by displaying family photographs and inviting parents to contribute items from home to include in the classroom interest areas. For example, empty cans and boxes from familiar food items in children's homes can be used to stock the house area's refrigerator and cupboards. Create a bulletin board or display space where children can post art projects or other work they'd like to share. Allow children to choose the items for display and change them often.

- If your students are successfully making choices and managing classroom materials and interest areas, think about adding one or two new areas to your environment. Base your additions on what you know about your children—their needs and interests. Would this be a good time to introduce the Writing Area? What about the sand and water table? Be sure to define the new areas clearly and label them in both English and Native language. Teach any procedures necessary for the smooth operation of new interest areas. And don't forget to introduce the new areas to parents, as well.

- Based on your observations of how children are using the interest areas, begin to introduce new materials to expand and extend their learning. Introduce the materials in Small Group Time or Circle Time and have the children help place them in the appropriate interest area. Think about adding materials that are a bit more complex and that will challenge and enhance children's experiences in the classroom. Be sure new materials are organized and labeled to support children's independent access and clean up.

- Continue to include literacy materials such as books and writing tools in each classroom interest area and reinforce their use as you interact with your students. As you begin the second quarter and periodically throughout the year, change out the available books and add new materials to maintain children's interest and curiosity.

Routines

The daily routine should be well-established by the second quarter and children should be comfortable moving from activity to activity throughout the day. Continue to refer to your routine cards or photographs as the day progresses and make plans for ways to introduce the routine to new children who may enroll at anytime during the year.

Children may be ready to spend a bit more time each day in **Circle Time** and teachers may be able to introduce some new activities. Observe children's behavior and their attention span and use that information to determine the appropriate length and content of Circle Time. If children are actively involved in read-alouds and are comfortable with basic interactive reading strategies, it may be time to introduce the more complex interactions of Dialogic Reading. Again, use what you know about your children and your observations of their behavior to guide the complexity of your Dialogic Reading prompts.

During the second quarter, teachers will complete the CIRCLES Development Checklist for each child based on their observations from the prior few months. If there are areas that have not been observed, create opportunities for observation in **Small Group Time**. For example, if teachers are lacking observations of children's mathematical thinking, they may want to design a Small Group Time session around sorting Counting Bears of differing colors and sizes, or around measuring tools in the sand/water table; or around gluing paper shapes on paper to create designs or pictures. By selecting appropriate materials, teachers can create opportunities to observe children's skills and thinking in specific areas from the Work Sampling System and the Preschool Standards.

During **Work Time**, both teachers will continue to be actively engaged with children in the interest areas, offering support when needed, facilitating conversation and reinforcing new learning and concepts. As their knowledge of their students grows, teachers will be more intentional about their interactions with children and will choose strategies designed to move children's learning to the next level.

The Wonder-Work-Share process can also be more complex as the year progresses. Rather than just pointing or naming an interest area in response to "I wonder where you will work today…." children should be encouraged to expand their response. To help children be more specific about their planning, teachers can ask "What will you do there?" or "What will you work with in the art area?" Following Work Time, open-ended questions can be used to encourage children to add details to their descriptions of what they did that day.

The beginning of the second quarter is a good time for the teacher and co-teacher to assess the effectiveness of all the routines in the classroom. Are there any times of the day that are problematic, or that seem to result in chaos or misbehaviors? If so, how might you make changes in your routines or procedures to effect positive change? Is there a mismatch between your expectations and children's abilities? Are there procedures that should be taught or re-taught to make things go more smoothly? Are the materials or activities being presented too easy or too challenging? Are children being asked to "wait" too long between activities? Are there activities that could make those transitions go more smoothly? Addressing challenges early in the year by analyzing and correcting problems in the daily routine is time well spent and a valuable investment in the efficient operation of your classroom.

Learning Communities

As learning communities grow and develop, comfort levels increase. The sense of predictability, belonging and security are well established by the second quarter, but that doesn't mean we don't still accommodate for each of them. Teachers still strive to be predictable with their routines, and continue to build those very important senses of belonging and security to the classroom every day.

As the Daily Routine becomes a more important part of the children's day, it is essential to build on those simple blocks of time, and help children transition from one block to another with intentionality.

As children become more used to the routine of Circle Time, expand the types of experiences provided (add some counting and/or letter activities, talk about the weather, use Dialogic Reading strategies while reading aloud, etc.), and increase the block of time by a few minutes.

Add these new items with intentionality. Have a purpose for each new segment you add to Circle Time. Make it meaningful for children. Individualize for children to make personal connections. For example, a familiar birthday song for a child, or reciting a rhyme that is a class favorite. Use children's names as much as possible. Have a child deliver the morning message, or point to the words while you deliver it. Establish the use of props during Circle Time. If Bonnie the Bumblebee puppet visits every day to share the morning message to the class, this becomes a more habitual and personal connection. The class adopts Bonnie as their own, and looks forward to seeing her every day.

Personalize your greetings and your good-byes with children, too. Having a special high-five for one child, and sharing a personal observation with another, makes those arrival and departure times special for all children

This intentionality and personalization becomes a part of everything you do and helps children develop a sense of familiarity. Consider how you can do this throughout the day. Here are some examples:

- *During Circle Time.* "Oh, I just looked at the lunch menu today. We're having our class favorite. What's our favorite lunch?" "Pizza and peaches!"
- *Name your class.* Have the children discuss and vote on their class name. Now, instead of being Miss Amy's students, the class takes on the ownership of being Deeno-Dinosaurs or Sky Hawks. Help children choose names that are meaningful and familiar to them or their community. The children are now connected by a common idea. They are a team.
- **Read a favorite class story** at rest time and spritz "resting sprinkles" for children who prefer it, to help them rest.

Assessments

Assessment during the second quarter of the year is focused on collecting the observations/anecdotal notes made to date, and analyzing information about each child's developmental levels, learning needs and interests.

Observation. Continue to be a good observer of children every day. Watch how children approach learning and tasks. Record anecdotal notes during this time so you have a written record of where children were at the beginning of the year, to compare with notes taken later in the year.

Screening. By the second quarter, screening should be completed on all children who were enrolled at the beginning of the year and parent conferences scheduled to discuss the results of all screenings. Any necessary referrals, evaluations and/or interventions should be in process.

CIRCLES Learning Domains Checklist. During the last half of this quarter, take time to complete the developmental checklist for each child. Using all of your available assessment data—observations, anecdotal notes, samples of work, and screening information—complete the forms.

Each form has a place to record a Fall and a Spring collection of data. Teachers can either check the box, or put a date in the box for when they are recording their assessment. For each indicator, the teacher should mark Beginning, Emerging, or Proficient, as defined below.

Beginning (Beg) = *The child is beginning to show the ability to do this skill, does it infrequently and inconsistently.*

Emergent (Emerg) = *The child shows emerging tendencies in her or her ability to do the skill, and completes it correctly more times than incorrectly.*

Proficient (Prof) = *The child is proficient or has mastered the skill, and does it correctly with frequency and consistency.*

When complete, review the forms and summarize briefly so you can share this information with parents. With parents, share

- At least one strength in 3-5 of the domain areas
- At least two areas for next steps
- One strategy in each of those two areas that parents can do at home to support their child's learning.

Lesson Planning

Teachers and co-teachers will continue to use the CIRCLES Daily Lesson Plan each week to establish learning goals, choose materials, and develop activities to meet the needs of children in the program. In the second quarter, teachers have more information on their children available through their observations and the completion of the CIRCLES Learning Domains (CLD) Checklist. This assessment information tells teachers what their students know and are able to do, and informs lesson planning that will support children in moving to the next level in their learning and development.

Teachers will use their assessment data to choose their instructional focus for the week. They will refer to the developmental domains and indicators on the CLD checklist and choose an appropriate focus from the CIRCLES Learning Domains for Children 3-5 Years.

Parent Engagement

As relationships and rapport with parents builds, teachers will offer increased opportunities for parents to engage with their children at school—and provide ideas for ways that parents can support their children's learning at home.

In the second quarter, form parent-teacher partnerships that support children's growth and development. Without trusting relationships, partnerships often fail. Building and keeping the relationship is important for parent-teacher collaboration. We know that relationship building takes time, which is why we recommend taking the time to culture and nurture the partnership in the first quarter, and build on the rapport you have already established with parents in the second quarter, and subsequently, throughout the year.

One way to do build this rapport is to encourage parents' active participation in onsite Parent Time and Parent and Child Together (PACT) Time® activities.

Here are some things to consider and do within this second quarter:

- Provide routine and consistent Parent Time sessions on topics of interest to parents—especially topics that support their engagement with their children's' learning achievement.
- Recognize that parent involvement comes at differing levels. Some parents are most comfortable at a volunteer stage of involvement. Other parents want to be in the classroom to work with their children (PACT Time). Another parent may be more comfortable helping to organize a learning field trip. Some may only be interested in parent engagement activities they can do at home. Invite parents to be involved at whatever level they are comfortable, especially at first, and help them to stretch and grow from there in their levels of engagement.

- Recognize that barriers to parent involvement can be challenging, and help parents to overcome those barriers. Talk to parents about roadblocks that keep them from being involved, and work to help them solve the issues.
- This quarter, create a few informal opportunities for parents to be involved in various ways. Help them to feel successful in however they choose to be involved.
- Provide at least one family night event a month and invite parent participation. Ask parents for their ideas and their help in planning.
- Plan a Transfer Home Idea for parents at least weekly. Provide the idea, the materials, and the support needed, in order for parents and children to be successful with the activity.
- Plan for a parent conference so teachers can meet one-on-one with parents to share information about their children's growth and development, screenings and assessments, and academic progress. Encourage questions and provide ways for parents to support their children in these areas of growth.

Quarter Three

Environment

When children return to school from winter break, they may welcome the familiarity of a classroom that hasn't undergone major changes since they left in December. They may also have to be reminded of a few routines and guidelines. Allow children time to ease back into the room and the routine before introducing new elements.

After a week or so, think about any new interest areas you might add to your classroom or areas that might be adapted in some way. Would a Discovery Area with plants or animals or nature items be an interesting addition? Is a Cooking Area a possibility where children might prepare their own snacks using a recipe with pictorial directions? Could the House Area be converted to a restaurant or a doctor's office or a grocery store?

Many teachers create "prop boxes" of materials around a particular theme that can be brought out and used to create a new environment in the classroom or outdoors that encourages a different type of creative dramatic play. For example, to change the House Area to a restaurant, a prop box might contain menus, order pads & pencils, aprons, a cash register, play money, tablecloths, etc. A camping prop box for outside play might include backpacks, a tent, flashlights, sleeping bags, binoculars, fishing poles, nature books, etc. Could you create prop boxes for other themes that might be familiar to your children, like a doctor's office? A hair salon? A post office?

Continue to monitor your students' developing skills and their use of classroom materials and interest areas. Using the guidelines discussed in Quarter 2, modify your centers or rotate materials to maintain interest and challenge children's learning.

Routines

Continue to follow the established daily routine for your classroom. Use the guidelines outlined in Quarter 2 to adapt lessons, activities and materials to challenge children's growing skills and set up opportunities as needed to observe all areas of their development.

Continue to add complexity to routines such as Dialogic Reading and Wonder-Work-Share as children's literacy skills become more advanced. Children may be ready to handle more advanced CROWD prompts during read-clouds that call for reflection and additional verbalization in their responses. Planning and sharing activities around Work Time can also be more complex, asking children for more verbal details and even beginning to represent their ideas in drawings or writing.

Learning Communities

Learning communities for children can extend beyond the classroom to include their families, other children in the school, and community members. While children grow and thrive in supportive classroom communities where they understand the expectations, and follow daily routines and habits, they flourish when their own ideas are put into practice as a tradition.

Sometimes routines and habits can turn into tradition when they are repeated time after time, and year after year. For example, the simple routine of starting the day with a good morning song, moves from a routine to a tradition when that sound is personalized for the class or students, and is done every single day. Instead of simply sing a generic good morning song, make it unique. "Good morning Jack, good morning, Jill, good morning everyone on the hill. Good morning Alex, good morning Sue, good morning to everyone and to you. Good morning Charlie, good morning Ray, it sure is good to see you today." And so on.

During this third quarter, think larger to create a new classroom tradition, or continue an existing one, and plan at least one traditional event. If the Sky Hawks class decides they want to have a "Donuts with Dad" breakfast this year, they do all of the planning and participate in carrying out the event. They decide the menu, make invitations, deliver them, plan table decorations, and a small program, if they want. If the "Donuts with Dad" event is repeated year after year, the class continues a tradition. Participating in events like this create teamwork and a sense of unity. They are also great parent involvement activities too!

Assessments

Assessment during the third quarter of the year continues to focus on ongoing observation and documentation through anecdotal notes and samples of student work. Children's performance is summarized again using the CIRCLES Learning Domains Checklist. In addition, oral language tests and required program assessments are often administered as mid-year assessments.

> **Observation.** Continue to be a good observer of children every day. Watch how children approach learning and tasks. Record anecdotal notes during this time so you have a written record of where children were at the beginning of the year until now.
>
> **CIRCLES Learning Domain Checklists.** During the third quarter, complete any CLD checklists that have not yet been completed as soon as possible in Quarter 3. Remember to schedule a parent conference.
>
> **Oral Language Test.** This vocabulary assessment is often given for the second time to all preschool children mid-winter.

Lesson Planning

Teachers and co-teachers continue to use the CIRCLES Daily Lesson Plan and complete weekly to establish learning goals, choose materials, and develop activities to meet the needs of children in the program. As described in the Quarter 2 guidelines, teachers will use their assessment data to choose their instructional focus for the week. They will refer to the learning domains the CLD Checklist information to choose an appropriate lesson plan focus.

Parent Engagement

Often times, parent engagement can be effectively supported by providing parent education. In CIRCLES, parent education is built into the program through the Parent Time and PACT Time components. Parent education supports parents as they reinforce their parenting skills, understand child development, and learn new strategies to support learning. This happens through informal conversations, workshops, written communication, one-on-one parent conferences, and a variety of appropriate means. It provides the tools parents need to support children's learning at school and at home.

PACT Time provides the classroom "lab" for parents where they can practice these newly learned skills from Parent Time, and try them out with their children in the classroom. Teachers support parents and provide guidance and additional ideas. The next step is for parents to take these strategies home.

Remember the main purpose for supporting parents' engagement with their children is to improve academic achievement and prepare children ready for school. We want parents to have skills they can use beyond the preschool classroom—skills they can use at home, and in later grades, with their children.

Home-school partnerships, when built on trust, can and do lead to high quality educational experiences that in turn improve schools, strengthen families, and prepare children for kindergarten.

In quarter three, continue to build relationships and rapport, increase the intensity of parent education workshops or family events, and focus directly on ways to support children's academic achievement.

- Provide a relaxed, positive experience for parents (and often parents and children together) in the school setting in order to support children's success in school.
- Provide parents with information on topics to enhance children's learning and engage parents in school events and activities such as:
    o   Preschool expectations
    o   How preschool children learn best
    o   What the preschool curriculum looks like

- How parents can be involved in children's learning
- Understanding specific learning strategies that children experience in the classroom
- Understanding early childhood standards and why they are important
- Understanding screening and assessment, and how teachers use these to plan experiences for children
- Learning strategies that parents can practice at home with their children to support their growth and development.

- Increase the engagement of parents in school activities/events to benefit children's school success
- Introduce parents unfamiliar with the school setting to a warm and "family friendly" school atmosphere.
- Recruit those parents "most in need" to more intensive education services offered in the school or community.

Quarter Four

Environment

During the last quarter of the school year, be sure that the classroom environment continues to be interesting and challenging for your students. Some children will be preparing to enter kindergarten in the fall and will be ready for more advanced materials. Perhaps the kindergarten teachers at your school are willing to loan manipulatives, games, or other resources that their children have "outgrown" but that would be perfect for your older four-year-olds at the end of the year. Your interest areas should continue to reflect the interests and developmental levels of all children in your classroom. When the weather is pleasant in the spring, extend learning into the outdoors, designing discovery, and exploratory activities that take advantage of access to the natural world.

Routines

Consider the ways you might adapt your routines for your older four-year-olds to introduce them to procedures they may encounter in the fall. Is it possible for them to visit a kindergarten classroom for story time or a special activity? Could a kindergarten "buddy" show them around the classroom? Could your class go to the kindergarten playground on occasion at the end of the year to explore what it has to offer? These kinds of activities can help ease the transition to kindergarten for children and their parents.

Learning Communities

By now, the children in your classroom have experienced the connectedness of their learning community. They understand the expectations of classroom routines, enjoy a sense of belonging within the community, and feel secure and safe in their preschool classroom environment.

In this quarter children and parents will begin thinking about the next steps—what happens beyond this year in preschool. Will the child be returning to preschool next year? Will the child transition to kindergarten and a new school?

Transitions can be tough for everyone but being part of a community can help ease the challenges. Parents and children together can participate in community-building activities and experiences to help make this transition as smooth as possible. Gradually introduce kindergarten transitioning students and their parents to the new classroom environment. As mentioned in the parent engagement section of this quarter, work to create a transition plan that supports children in leaving their old community behind, and moving forward to a new community. This will take time, so the plan should start small and gradually build. It is important not to start too early, or to wait too long. Children need time and support to grapple with the idea of leaving a place where they feel secure, and moving on to the next phase of their academic years.

Some transition activities that help to bridge the gap between new communities could be:

- Visiting the new classroom when it is empty to see what it looks like. Take a walk from the current classroom to the new one, to see how far away (or how close!) it is.
- Visit the classroom Circle Time for 10-15 minutes so children can observe the other children, and especially the teacher, in action.
- Invite parents to be a part of these classroom visitations.
- Plan a joint event activity with kindergarten students, such as a field trip or parent night, so both parents and children have opportunities to meet and interact with their future teachers.
- Plan a transition/graduation ceremony and include the Kindergarten teacher in the event.

Assessments

The end-of-the-year assessments are a final measure of what children have learned. During the fourth quarter, multiple assessments are given and can provide valuable information to inform placement decisions for the following year. Be sure to conference with parents to share final assessment results.

Observation. Continue to be a good observer of children every day. Watch how children approach learning and tasks. Record anecdotal notes during this time so you have a written record of where children were at the beginning of the year, and at the end of the year. These notes are important data to show children's growth in specific areas.

CIRCLES Learning Domain Checklists. During the fourth quarter, teachers and co-teachers will again use their observations, anecdotal notes and examples of children's work to complete the **CLD Checklists**. Refer to the guidelines for Quarter 2 to mark the performance indicators on the Checklist and complete share with parents.

Oral Language Test. This vocabulary assessment is sometimes given for the third time to all preschool children in the spring to check progress in expressive language development.

Formal Assessment. Many programs or schools will administer a formal, standardized assessment to students in the late winter or spring annually.

Lesson Planning

Teachers and co-teachers continue to use the CIRCLES Daily Lesson Plan and complete weekly to establish learning goals, choose materials, and develop activities to meet the needs of children in the program. As described in the Quarter 2 guidelines, teachers will use their assessment data to choose their instructional focus for the week. They will refer to the learning domains the CLD Checklist information to choose an appropriate lesson plan focus.

All areas of the CIRCLES Learning Domains will have been appropriately addressed by the end of the school year.

Parent Engagement

Successful parent engagement happens when schools, parents, and children form unique and equal partnerships in order to support children's learning—at home and at school. In this quarter, parents continue to use the strategies and knowledge gained in parent engagement activities to support their children's learning at home. One strong goal for parents is to provide a supportive home learning environment that promotes student success.

Encourage parents to extend learning from school to home. Parents can:

- Understand the work happening in the classroom and support that learning at home
- Seek out ways to provide additional support
- Provide extra experiences that support children's learning.
- Provide children with background knowledge on many subjects
- Create family times for such things as storytelling, sharing culture, family events, cooking together, discussing current topics, solving family problems.
- Take advantage of everyday routines and daily experiences to create learning experiences (e.g. grocery shopping, mailing a letter, planting a garden)

In this fourth quarter of the school year, parents are likely more experienced, and more confident, in how they engage with their children. Activities and strategies discussed in the previous quarters continue; however, we also look for parents to provide more leadership within the classroom and school.

As parents become more involved in their children's school experiences, they become confident leaders, and often mentors. Involve parents in decision-making, providing them with a voice. Include them on school leadership teams when they are ready to contribute. As parents become leaders and mentors in the school, they build capacity within the school to support ongoing parent engagement efforts.

In quarter four, some important activities to plan for parents include:

- A parent conference to discuss children's academic achievement, success toward meeting goals, and areas to continue to work on. Provide support for parents in the areas of growth and concern, so that parents can help focus on supporting their children at home.
- For the parents of children who are transitioning to Kindergarten next year, begin discussing this transition process. Work with the parent to create a transition plan that works for child, parent and teacher. Involve the kindergarten teacher in these discussions.
- Plan a Parent Time topic about Kindergarten transition and invite the Kindergarten teacher to share expectations.

Program Transitions

Transitions happen frequently in our lives. We move to a new home, change schools or jobs, bring a new children or spouse into our lives, and more. How we prepare for, and handle, these life transitions can often lay the groundwork for how successful the transition will ultimately be.

For young children of preschool age, the important transitions happen when children enter preschool, and when they leave. Enrolling into a new school, and meeting a new teacher and classmates, should be a fun for children. Unfortunately, sometimes the transition is met with apprehension and anxiety—on the part of both child and parent.

Creating seamless and effective transitions can't happen without family involvement, a support team, and planning. We all want children to succeed in school, so pulling the appropriate team together, and planning ahead is critical to that success.

Involve the Family

Transitions can be an emotional time for parents and the family, as well as for the child. Involve the family from the beginning, allowing plenty of time for the parent to get used to the idea of transition. Consult with parents ahead of time to share and discuss questions, uncover their anxieties about enrolling their child, and create a plan to move forward. Allow plenty of time for parents and children to get used to the idea of school, and provide any guidance or support requested to help ensure the family will be ready, when the appropriate time comes.

The Transition Team

Parent and family input is always the first step in transition. The other team members may vary depending on the child and family. A child enrolling in preschool for the first time may have a home visitor or parent educator, the preschool teacher, and school administrator on their transition team, as well as the parents of the child. A child with special needs, either entering or exiting the program, may also have a Special Education representative or an interventionist on their team. Children transitioning into a kindergarten program would likely have the addition of the kindergarten teacher, and perhaps an administrator or guidance counselor from the new school. At times, other community members may be involved, as needed, in helping a child and family during this transition process.

Planning

Planning should start early and be consistent. How often the transition team meets will depend on the plan that is created. A carefully planned transition is important for everyone involved, in order to:

- Prevent an interruption of services
- Provide families with opportunities to be partners in the transition process
- Facilitate the adjustment of children and parents to a new learning environment
- Eliminate the duplication of screenings
- Provide families with accurate enrollment and eligibility requirements
- Decrease stress caused by changes that families will experience
- Reduce fears of the unknown
- Help families and staff build relationships (Effective Transitions in FACE, Bureau of Indian Education, Family and Child Education).

For downloadable tools, templates, and additional content related to the CIRCLES® Curriculum Approach please visit our website at **familieslearning.org/our-solutions/circles.html**

CIRCLES®

A Culturally Appropriate Preschool Curriculum for American Indian Children

Contact the National Center for Families Learning (NCFL) for all of your CIRCLES® and Early Childhood Professional Development needs.

The complete CIRCLES® Curriculum Approach

Book 1: The Core Curriculum Approach

Book 2: Language & Literacy Development in Preschool
- Oral Language Development
- Phonological Awareness
- Alphabet Knowledge
- Writing in Preschool

Book 3: Family Engagement in Preschool

NCFL has designed a suite of professional development opportunities for early childhood educators to support the needs of your school or program that can include:

- Customization for your program
- Written curriculum materials
- On-site Consultation & Professional Development
- Online Professional Development & Support
- Technical Assistance & Coaching
- Family Event Support

For more information about the **CIRCLES Curriculum, CIRCLES Professional Development**, or to bring the CIRCLES Curriculum to your early childhood/preschool program, please contact the National Center for Families Learning, 502-584-1133 or visit our website at familieslearning.org.

REFERENCES

Bowman, B.T., Donavan, M.S., & Burns, M.S. (Eds.) (2001). *Eager to learn: Educating our preschoolers.* Washington DC: National Academy Press.

Brofenbrenner, U. (1979). *The ecology of human development: Experiments by nature and design.* Cambridge: Harvard University Press.

Clark, G. J. (2010). *The relationship between handwriting, reading, fine motor and visual-motor skills in kindergarteners.* Retrieved from http://lib.dr.iastate.edu/cgi/viewcontent.cgi?article=2432&context=etd

Dickenson, D.K., & Tabors, P.O. (2001). *Beginning literacy with language: Young children at home and school.* Baltimore: P.H. Brookes.

Epstein, J.L., Sanders, M.G., Simon, B.S., Salinas, K.C., Jansorn, N.R., & Van Voorhis, F.L. (2002). *School, family and community partnerships: Your handbook for action.* Thousand Oaks, CA: Corwin Press.

Epstein, J.L., Sanders, M.G., Simon, B.S., Salinas, K.C., Jansorn, N.R., & Van Voorhis, F.L. (2009). *School, family and community partnerships: Your handbook for action* (3rd ed.). Thousand Oaks, CA: Corwin Press.

Epstein, J.L., & Salinas, K.C. (2004, May). Schools as learning communities. *Educational Leadership*, 61(8), 12-18.

Gardiner, H. (1983). *Frames of mind.* New York: Basic Books.

Girolametto, L., Pearce, P.S., & Weitzman, E. (1996). Interactive focused stimulation for toddlers with expressive vocabulary delays. *Journal of Speech and Hearing Research*, 39, 1274-1283.

Goin, L. (1999). Planning academic programs for American Indian success: Learning strategies workshop. In *Indigenous education around the world: Workshop papers from the world Indigenous people's conference: Education.* (Albuquerque, NM, June 15-22, 1996).

Hamilton, M. (1977). Social learning and the transition from babbling to initial words. *The Journal of Genetic Psychology*, 130, 211-220.

Hart, B., & Risely, T.R. (1995). *Meaningful differences in the everyday experience of young American children.* Baltimore: P.H. Brookes.

Henderson, A.T., & Mapp, K.L. (2002). *A new wave of evidence: The impact of school, family, and community connections on student achievement.* Austin, TX: National Center for Family & Community Connections with Schools: Southwest Educational Development Laboratory.

Henderson, A.T., Mapp, K.L., Johnson, V.R., & Davies, D. (2007). *Beyond the bake sale: The essential guide to family-school partnerships.* New York, NY: The New Press.

Hilberg, R.S., & Tharp, R.G. (2002). *Theoretical perspectives, research findings, and classroom implications of the learning styles of American Indian and Alaska Native Students.* Charleston, WV: ERIC Clearinghouse in Rural Education and Small Schools. (ERIC Document Reproduction Service No. ED468000).

Hutchings, D.J., Greenfeld, M.D., & Epstein, J.L. (2008). *Family reading night.* Davidsonville, MD: Eye on Education, Inc.

Jacobs, K. (2004). Parent and child together time. In B.H. Wasik (Ed.), *Handbook of family literacy* (pp. 193-213). New Jersey: Lawrence Erlbaum Associations, Inc.

Jeynes, W. (2011). *Parental involvement and academic success.* New York: Routledge.

LaFromboise, T. D., Hoyt, D. R., Oliver, L., and Whitbeck, L. B. (2006). Family, community, and school influences on resilience among American Indian adolescents in the upper midwest. *Journal of Community Psychology.*, 34: 193–209. doi:10.1002/jcop.20090

Levesque, J. (2013). *Meta analysis of the studies of high performing family literacy programs.* National Center for Families Learning. Retrieved from: http://familieslearning.org/pdf/NCFL_Family_Engagement_Brief_.pdf

More, A.J. (1999). *Learning styles of Native Americans and Asians.* Paper presented at the 98th Annual Meeting of the American Psychology Association, Boston, MA, August 13, 1990. (ERIC Document Reproduction Service No. ED330535).

More, A.J. (1993). *Adapting teaching to the learning styles of Native Indian students.* (ERIC Document Reproduction Service No. ED366493).

Morgan, H. (2009). *What every teacher needs to know to teach Native American students.* Multicultural Education: Caddo Gap Press (16)4, 10-12.

National Center for Families Learning. (2009, 2015). *What works: An introductory teacher guide for early language and emergent literacy instruction.* Louisville, KY: Author.

National Early Literacy Panel. (2008). *Developing early literacy: Report of the National Early Literacy Panel.* Washington, DC: National Institute for Literacy.

Paradis, J., Genesee, F., & Crago, M. (2011). *Dual language development and disorders: A handbook on bilingualism and second language learning* (2nd Edition). Baltimore, MD: Brookes.

Pewewardy, C.D. (2002). Learning styles of American Indian/Alaska Native Students: A review of the literature and implications for practice. *Journal of American Indian Education*, 41(3).

Peweardy, C.D. (2008). Learning styles of American Indian/Alaska Native students. In J. Noel (Ed.), *Classic edition sources: Multicultural education* (pp. 1160121). New York: McGraw-Hill.

Pianta, R.C. (1999). *Enhancing relationships between teachers and children.* Washington, DC: American Psychological Association.

Price, M., Kallam, M., & Love, J. (2009). *The learning styles of Native American students and implications for classroom practice.* Southeastern Oklahoma State University. Retrieved from: http://www.se.edu/nas/files/2013/03/NAS-2009-Proceedings-M-Price.pdf

Research and Training Associates. (2004). Bureau of Indian Education, Family and Child Education Program, 2004 Impact Study. Overland Park, KS: Author.

Research and Training Associates. (2008). Bureau of Indian Education, Family and Child Education Program. Overland Park, KS: Author.

Research and Training Associates. (2010). Bureau of Indian Education, Family and Child Education Program. Overland Park, KS: Author.

Research and Training Associates. (2015). Bureau of Indian Education, Family and Child Education Program. Overland Park, KS: Author.

Red Horse, J.G., (1980). Family structure and value orientation in American Indians. *Social Casework: The Journal of Contemporary Social Work.* Retrieved from: http://www.dhs.state.mn.us/main/groups/children/documents/pub/dhs16_180056.pdf

Robertson, S.B., & Weismer, S.E. (1999). Effects of treatment on linguistic and social skills in toddlers with delayed language development. *Journal of Speech, Language, and Hearing Research, 42,* 1234-1248.

Schickendanz, J.A., (1999). *Much more than the ABCs: The early stages of reading and writing.* Washington, DC: National Association for the Education of Young Children.

Shonkoff, J.P., & Phillips, D.A. (Eds.). (2000). *From neurons to neighborhoods: The science of early childhood development.* Washington, DC: National Academy Press.

Smith, C., & Fluck, M. (2000). (Re-) Constructing pre-linguistic interpersonal processes to promote language development in young children with deviant or delayed communication skills. *British Journal of Educational Psychology, 70,* 369-389.

St. Charles, J., & Costantino, M. (2000). *Reading and the Native American learner: Research report.* Olympia, WA: Washington Office of the State Superintendent of Public Instruction, Office of Indian Education. (ERIC Document Reproduction No. ED451026).

Swisher, K. (1991). *American Indian/Alaska Native learning styles: Research and practice.* Charleson, WV: ERIC Clearinghouse on Rural Education and Small Schools. (ERIC Document Reproduction No. ED335175).

Tabors, P.O. (1997). *One child, two languages: A guide for preschool educators of children learning English as a second language.* Baltimore: P.H. Brookes.

Vygotsky, L., (1986). *Thought and Language.* In A. Kozulin (Ed. and Trans.), Cambridge: MIT Press.